Dynamic Progr

for

Coding Interviews

Kamal Rawat

Meenakshi

The Authors have taken care in editing this book, but we are humans and there may still be some errors or omissions in this book. We make no expressed or implied warranty of any kind for errors or omissions. No liability is assumed for incidental or consequential damage in connection with or arising out of the use of the information contained herein.

For comments, suggestion or feedback, please drop an email to:

hikrawat@gmail.com
meenakshighangas@gmail.com

ISBN: 9798386441050

DEDICATED TO

Shri Maha Singh Ghangas

CONTENTS

PREFACE

I have been teaching students 'How to prepare for Coding and System Design Interviews' for more than a decade now.

A Data Structure problem, such as reversing a linked list or implementing a thread safe Queue, is relatively simple to solve because there are theoretical references to start with. Dynamic Programming (DP) encompasses the most difficult types of problems asked in Coding Interviews at top-IT companies like Alphabet, Amazon, Meta, Microsoft, and others.

Even experienced coders have struggled to solve DP problems, even though most DP problems do not require knowledge of complex data structures or design patterns. All you need is the right strategy, a systematic approach, and a lot of practice.

While solving a problem, the solution is first visualized in the mind before it takes formal shape of an Algorithm that finally translates into code. DP problems are not easy to visualize in the head and hence not easy to solve.

DP is not a single algorithm, but rather a technique for optimising a solution (typically) given in the form of recursion. It applies to recursions that solve the same subproblem multiple times. Such recursions typically take exponential time, and DP can be used to visualise the logic of recursion in the opposite direction (bottom-up), eliminating not only overlapping subproblems but also recursion itself. In a nutshell (loosely speaking), DP is a method of optimising recursion. This approach will be very counter-intuitive if not combined with recursion.

This book is written with the intention that if a teacher read it, he will make dynamic programming very interesting to his students. If a developer has this book, he should be very confident in answering algorithm questions in any interview. In addition, anyone who reads it will gain a tool for approaching problems in coding competitions.

Being a good coder is not about learning a programming language, it is about mastering the art of problem solving.

How to read this book

This book is divided into two parts. The first part has three chapters and the second has five chapters. The first part gradually introduces the reader to the concepts and then discusses the strategy that can be used to solve any Dynamic Programming problem.

The second part talks about multiple ways of approaching the Dynamic programming solution of a problem. Each chapter in the second part provides a different way of looking at the problem. We tried to bucketize the DP problems, but the division is not mutually exclusive. A path problem (chapter-4) can be approached from the point-of-view of the number of variables in the problem (chapter-5) and it may be a variation of greedy (chapter-7) where you explore all possible outcomes (Chapter-6).

Even if you are an expert in Dynamic Programming and can solve hard problems, I will suggest you read at least the Chapter-3 of the first part before reading the second part. If you have time, please read the book from cover-to-cover. I am sure it will add value to your problem-solving abilities.

PART-1

CONCEPTS & STRATEGY

The first part of this book has three chapters that cover everything required for concept building of Dynamic Programming with suitable examples. Once you finish reading this part, you should be able to implement DP algorithms on your own and will be able to discuss DP on any forum.

DP is a technique to improve a specific kind of recursive solution. In the foundations of Dynamic Programming, is the logic that comes straight from Recursion. Therefore, if you want to become an expert in DP, start with building expertise in recursive logic building. Our first chapter is entirely dedicated to Recursion. The second chapter decodes all the mysterious phrases surrounding DP and provides a conceptual and easy explanation of all keywords. The third chapter takes a few DP examples and attempts to develop a strategy that may be applied to solve any DP problem.

However, problem-solving in computer is like mathematics. Knowing the concepts and learning the theorems is not enough. We must practice sufficiently to develop metal templates that help us solve any DP problem. The second part is dedicated to that.

Recursion, and what it looks like inside memory.

Recursion

Most computer concepts have their roots in Mathematics, and Recursion is no exception. You've probably encountered equations like the one below in your high school math.

$$\sum n \begin{cases} = n + \sum (n-1) & \text{If } n>1 \\ = 1 & \text{If } n=1 \end{cases} \qquad Sum(n) \begin{cases} = n + Sum(n\text{-}1) & \text{If } n>1 \\ = 1 & \text{If } n=1 \end{cases}$$

Recursion in Mathematics

It is read as "**Sum** *of first* **n** *numbers is equal to* **n** *plus* **Sum** *of first* **(n−1)** *numbers, except when* **n** *is* **1**, *in which case* **Sum (1)** *has a fixed value,* **1**". **n,** being a positive integer. Function Sum is defined in terms of Sum itself. This is called Recursion.

In computer programming, *"when a function calls itself either directly or indirectly, it is called a Recursive Function and the process is called Recursion"*.

Typically, the function performs a portion of the task, and the remainder is delegated to one or more recursive calls of the same function; thus, multiple instances of the same function exist in memory, each performing a portion of the overall task. When a terminating condition (also known as a Base condition) is reached, the function stops calling itself.

> Recursion is a problem-solving technique in which the solution to a larger problem is defined in terms of smaller instances of itself.

Writing recursive code is not as difficult as it may appear, in fact, in most cases it is relatively simpler because we are solving only part of the overall problem and not the complete problem. Writing recursive code is a two-step process,

1. Visualize the recursion by defining larger solution in terms of smaller solutions of the exact same type, and,

2. Include one or more terminating conditions.

If we translate the previous example of calculating the sum of first n positive integers from mathematics to a programming language syntax, we will get the following code.

Example 1.1: Function for calculating the sum of the first n positive numbers:

```
int sum(unsigned int n){
  if(n == 1)
    return 1;
  else
    return n + sum(n-1);
}
```
Code: 1.1

As a good coding practice, always check your program against the boundary values of input parameters. This code, in C++, contains a bug. When you call the function for n=0,

```
sum(0);
```

it will act in an undefined manner. The terminating condition (n==1) will be skipped, and the code will enter an unguarded recursion, calling the function for n = -1 and leaving the result undefined[1].

We should train our eyes to spot and fix such issues in our code, especially during the whiteboard interview when there is no compiler to catch our errors. You are expected to be a good code reviewer even if you are not a developer and are in an Engineering Manager or Software Development Manager profile. The final code is as follows:

```
int sum(unsigned int n){
  if(n == 0) // First terminating condition
    return 0;

  if(n == 1) // Second terminating condition
    return 1;

  return n + sum(n-1);
}
```

Code: 1.2

Above function can be written in a more compact form:

```
int sum(unsigned int n){
  return (n==0||n==1)? n: (n+sum(n-1));
}
```

Code: 1.3

Which of the two codes will you prefer to write?

Some coders have an undue bias toward writing compact code (with fewer lines of code), which is especially true during the interview. They may believe writing such code will impress the interviewer, or they may have a habit of writing such code. However, compact code is often obfuscated and difficult to maintain. One thumb rule for writing good code is,

"Whenever there is a choice between simple and obfuscated code, go for simpler one, unless

---

[1] Conversion from signed to unsigned is not defined for negative numbers in C++. For example, the value of y in the following code is not defined:

```
int x = -1;
unsigned int y = x;
```

the other one has clear performance or memory advantage."

And this rule does not apply only to interviews. Many people on the team read the code we write. Developers come and go, but the code is there to stay for decades. The code I wrote in both Adobe and Microsoft merged with code written many years ago, and now someone else must be writing code on top of my code. The easier it is for others to understand and maintain, the better.

If you are writing code on paper or a whiteboard during an interview, write the code spaciously, it provides some space for you to correct the mistakes there itself, because there is more white space on the paper. The rule is only for empty space in the code and choosing between two conditions doing exactly same work. A check should never be omitted for the sake of simplicity, clarity, or extra space on the paper.

Never-Ever miss any terminating condition.

While writing a recursive function, you must define three things:

i.   Work done by each function,

ii.   Work delegated to recursion, and

iii.   Terminating condition(s).

In Code 1.1, the function adds n to the summation of (n−1), but the responsibility of computing summation of (n−1) is delegated to recursion.

```
int sum(unsigned int n)
{
    if( n == 1)         ⎤→ TERMINATING
        return 1;       ⎦    CONDITION
    else                    → WORK DONE BY FUNCTION
        return n + sum(n-1);
}                              ↳ WORK DELEGATED
                                  TO RECURSION
```

Question 1.1: Following is the definition of Factorial for non-negative integers:

```
Fact(n) = n * Fact(n-1)     if n>1
        = 1                 if n =1
```

Write both recursive and non-recursive function to find factorial of n.

Question 1.2: Given an array, `arr`, of integers, write a recursive function that add sum of all the previous numbers to each index of the array. For example, if input array is

   {1, 2, 3, 4, 5, 6}

Then, your function should change it to

   {1, 3, 6, 10, 15, 21}

The functions in Example 1.1 are to demonstrate recursion. You may very well write a non-recursive function using a loop to compute the sum of n numbers as shown below:

```
int sum(int n){
    int res = 0;
    for(int i=1; i<=n; i++)
        res += i;
    return res;
}
```

Code: 1.4

We should pay attention to the following four things (in this order) while writing a function:

1. It should **serve the purpose**. The function must always return expected results for every possible test case. It should not be ambiguous for any input.

2. It should take a **minimum of time** to execute.

3. It should consume **minimum extra memory** while executing.

4. The Function should be **simple to comprehend**. The code should ideally be self-explanatory enough that no documentation (comments) is required.

We should not care much about lines of code in a function during coding (or during the interview) and there is no code duplication.

We will later discover that a recursive solution requires more time and memory than an iterative solution. If both iterative and recursive solutions are equally easy to code (like in Example 1.1), we should always choose a non-recursive solution.

 INTERVIEW TIP
 Write the iterative solution whenever recursive and non-recursive (non-recursive)

solutions are equally simple to code. It typically outperforms the recursive solution.

Therefore, if you can solve a problem non-recursively, it is not advisable to write the recursive code for it. The issue, however, is that it might be extremely challenging, if not impossible, to find a non-recursive solution for many problems. Most Binary tree, Graph, and Backtracking problems are solved recursively. Later in this book, we will discover that even Dynamic programming is nothing more than an optimization of recursion. Therefore, whether we like it or not, we must master the art of designing recursive solutions. Let's look at one more example,

Example 1.2: Recursion to compute n[th] power of a number x is:

$$x^n \begin{cases} = x * x^{n-1} & \text{If } n >= 1 \\ = 1 & \text{If } n = 0 \end{cases} \qquad Pow(x, n) \begin{cases} = Pow(x, n\text{-}1) & \text{If } n >= 1 \\ = 1 & \text{If } n = 0 \end{cases}$$

Above equation assumes n to be a non-negative integer. When we translate logic to code, we should make sure that the code works for all values of the input parameter and handles all possibilities explicitly without assuming anything.

```
int power(int x, int n){
    if(0 == x || 1 == x)  // 1st TEMINATING CONDITION
        return x;
    if(2 == x)            // 2nd TEMINATING CONDITION
        return 1<<n;
    if(0 == n)            // 3rd TERMINATING CONITION
        return 1;
    else
        return x * power(x, n-1);
}
```

Code: 1.5

In the above code, the recursive function has two inputs. One of them, n changes and terminates the recursion, while the other, x remains constant across the function calls. The first terminating condition prevents unnecessary function calls when x is 0 or 1.

nth-Power-of-two can be directly computed by left-shifting the binary representation of 1 by n positions, the second terminating condition, is to find power-of-two in constant time. Even if we do not put this condition, the code will still be correct, but adding this condition makes the code run in constant time for x = 2.

Code 1.5 is not the most optimal way to find the power, it takes O(n) time. In most libraries the power function is implemented as lg(n) time function where the result is multiplied with itself to double the power as shown below:

```
int power(int x, int n){
    if(0 == x || 1 == x){ return x; }
    if(2 == x){ return 1<<n; }
    if(0 == n)return 1;
    int res = power(x, n/2);
    if(n%2 == 0)
        return res * res;
    else
        return res * res * x;
}
```

Code: 1.6

The benefit of recursion is that it makes it quite simple to envision a solution that would otherwise be very difficult to understand. In Recursion, only a portion of the problem needs to be solved; the rest can be defined in terms of recursion itself. Consider the following example:

Example 1.3 (Tower of Hanoi): Tower of Hanoi is a Mathematical Game. There are three rods, Source, Destination, and Extra marked as S, D, and E respectively. There are n discs, each of different sizes, which can be inserted into any one of these three rods. All discs are initially inserted in the Source rod in the decreasing order (smallest at the top), as shown in the following diagram for n=4 discs.

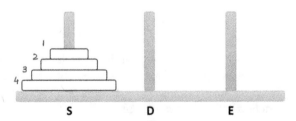

Print all the steps required to move all discs from Source rod (S) to the Destination rod (D). Following diagram shows the final state.

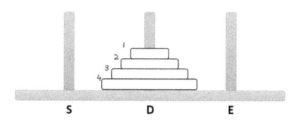

While moving discs, there are two constraints:

i.   Only one disc at a time can be moved.
ii. At no point during the process should a larger disc be placed on top of a smaller disc.

Write a function that accept characters representing names of three rods (S, D & E respectively) and the number of discs (n) and print the movement of discs between rods as they move from the initial state (inside S) to the final state (inside D). Following is the signature of the function,

```
/* s, d, e: Names of three rods, n: # of discs*/
void towerOfHanoi(char s, char d, char e, int n)
```

One of the most important steps in creating a recursive solution is correctly defining and reading the function signature. This may appear to be a difficult problem to solve otherwise, but if we think recursively, we can solve it in following three simple steps.

Step-1: Move n-1 discs from S to E using D as Extra

Let us assume that somehow n-1 discs are moved from S to E. If needed D may be used as an extra rod to accomplish this. This problem of, "moving n-1 discs from S to E using D", is similar to the original problem of, "moving n discs from S to D using E". After Step-1, the discs are as shown in the following figure:

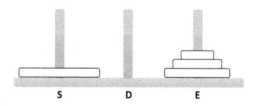

Step-2: Move the n'th disc from S to D

Move the last disc, Disc No. n, from S to D. This is a single step of execution and can performed by directly printing to the console

```
System.out.println("Move "+n" FROM "+s+" TO "+e);
```

Step-3: Move n-1 discs from E to D using S as extra

This problem is similar to Step-1 which was similar to the original problem. Only parameters are different.

Step-1 and Step-3, being problems of the same type, can be solved by making recursive calls to the same function. Following is the recursive function for Tower of Hanoi:

```
void towerOfHanoi(char s, char d, char e, int n){
    if(n <= 0)       // TERMINATING CONDITION
        return;
    towerOfHanoi(s, e, d, n-1);
    System.out.println("Move "+n+" FROM "+s+" TO "+d);
    towerOfHanoi(e, d, s, n-1);
}
```

Code: 1.7

The recursion in above code terminates when there is no disk (n==0). The terminating condition in the code is "less-than-or-equal-to", so that the function is capable of handling negative n.

The function first delegates the responsibility to "move n-1 discs from S to E" and later to "move n-1 discs from E to D" to the recursive calls of itself. Moving the nth disc from S to D is the sole responsibility of a function.

The terminating (base) condition of recursion is almost always in terms of input parameters. Think like this, when will the input parameter result in a situation of no-work-done by the function. When you call the function for 3 discs (n=3)

```
towerOfHanoi('s', 'd', 'e', 3);
```

It will result in the following output

```
Move Disk-1 FROM s TO d
Move Disk-2 FROM s TO e
Move Disk-1 FROM d TO e
Move Disk-3 FROM s TO d
Move Disk-1 FROM e TO s
Move Disk-2 FROM e TO d
Move Disk-1 FROM s TO d
```

Can you solve the Tower-of-Hanoi problem for 10 discs on your own? Most likely not! But you wrote the code that can solve it for you.

Typically, the first step in computer problem-solving is to logically solve the problem entirely in our mind, after which that logic is converted into code. Although we may not be able to logically solve the Tower-of-Hanoi problem for 10 discs in our mind, we have written the code to do so. This is the power of recursion; it helps us solve a problem without fully solving it. It shows how powerful recursion can be, even if it takes more time and more memory.

Tail Recursion

If a recursive function calls itself only once, and that too in its last statement after performing what it must perform, it is called Tail-Recursion. Following code to traverse and print a linked list is an example of tail-recursion.

```
void traverse(Node head){
  if(head != null){
    System.out.print(head.data);
    traverse(head.next);
  }
}
```

If head of the following linked list is passed as parameter to above function:

Input: **Output:**

   1 2 3 4

The `traverse` function prints the list in forward order.

In most cases, it is very easy to re-write a tail recursion in form of a loop.

```
void traverse(Node head){
  while(head != null){
    System.out.print(head.data);
    head = head.next;
  }
}
```

One of the most pervasive forms of recursion is seen in binary tree algorithms. Consider the code to print the In-Order traversal of a Binary tree. The in-order traversal first traverse left subtree in in-order, then print the data at root of the tree and finally traverse the right subtree in in-order.

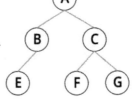

Algorithm:
1. Traverse Root
2. Traverse Left SubTree in PreOrder
3. Traverse Right SubTree in PreOrder

Output:
   A B E C F G

If structure of the Node is:

```
class Node{
  Node left;      // Pointer to Left subtree
  int data;
  Node right;     // Pointer to Right subtree
};
```

Following is the function to print In-Order traversal of a tree:

```
void inOrder(Node r){
  if(r == null)
    return;

  inOrder(r.left);
  System.out.print(r.data);
  inOrder(r.right);
}
```

Code: 1.9

The recursion in above code cannot be termed as tail recursion, even though it has a recursive call at the end of the function.

The function in Code 1.9 terminates when r becomes null. It will result in extra function calls because function will be called for left and right children even when they are null. A better solution is to make the recursive call only when the child is not null.

```
void inOrder(node r){
  if(r == NULL)
    return;
  if(r.left != NULL){ inOrder(r.left); }
  System.out.print(r.data);
  if(r.right != NULL){ inOrder(r.right); }
}
```

Code: 1.10

Output of the previous two codes is the same. The small checks in Code 1.10 may appear to be unnecessary, if not an overhead, but they will cut the total number of function calls by half. This is due the fact that total number of null pointers in a Binary tree is n+1, where n is the number of nodes in that tree. The binary tree with 7 nodes below has 8 null pointers.

Children of all the leaf nodes, right child of E and left child of C are all nulls.

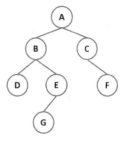

If we count a pointer to the root as one pointer, we get a total of seven non-null pointers.

Including such checks in the code not only optimises it, but also demonstrates your meticulous code-review skills and commitment to writing better code.

How to solve a problem using recursion.

Coding interviews test your problem-solving and expect the final solution to be as code in your preferred programming language. With recursion, it is possible to solve a problem without completely solving it. You need to define the solution of a larger problem in terms of the solution of smaller problems of the same type.

This method of problem-solving in which you focus on only one part of the problem and delegate the rest will start coming naturally to you once you get the hold of recursion. In Binary tree problems, for example, we focus on solving the problem for the root node and delegate solving the problem for left and right subtrees to recursion. The recursion strategy is to Define, Delegate, and Add, as shown in the diagram below:

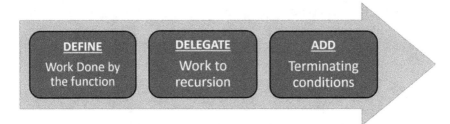

We all know about Bubble Sort, where an array is sorted in n passes as shown in the following code:

```
void bubbleSort(int[] arr){
  int n = arr.length;
  while( n > 1 ){
    for(int i=0; i<n-1; i++){
      if(arr[i] > arr[i+1])
        swap(arr, i, i+1);
    }
    n--;
  }
}
```

Code: 1.11

Where swap is a function that swaps two elements of an integer array.

```
void swap(int[] a, int i, int j){
  int temp = a[i];
  a[i] = a[j];
  a[j] = temp;
}
```

Each iteration of outer while loop of bubble sort pushes the largest element of the current array of size n to its last position, i.e n-1. After every pass the size of current array is decrement. When this size becomes 1 the loop terminated because single-element array is already sorted. If input array is

9, 6, 2, 12, 11, 9, 3, 7

The largest element, 12, will reach the end of array after the first pass:

6, 2, 9, 11, 9, 3, 7, **12**

With 12 at the last position, now sort the first n-1 elements. The two problems, "*Sort first n elements*" and "*Sort first n-1 elements*" are exactly same problems with different parameters.

Recursive implementation of Bubble Sort:

We can define a function that pushes the largest element of the current array (of size n) to its last position and then delegate the responsibility of sorting rest of the array (of size n-1) to recursion.

```
void bubbleSortRec(int *arr, int n){
  if(n <= 1){ return; }
  for(int i=0; i<n-1; i++){
    if(arr[i] > arr[i+1])
      swap(arr, i, i+1);
  }
  bubbleSortRec(arr, n-1);
}
```

Code: 1.12

We cannot be good coders unless we master the art of recursion. My advice to anyone reading this book is to try to implement simple programs like linear search, binary search, sorting, and so on recursively. It will be an excellent net practice session before the actual match.

Question 1.3: Below code prints the mathematical table of n.

```
void printTable(int n){
  for(int i=1; i<=10; i++){
    System.out.println( n + " * "+i+" = "+(n*i));
  }
}
```

Code: 1.13

Write a recursive function that prints the mathematical table of n.

Hint: You may have to pass/accept i as parameter.

Memory Model – How it looks inside memory.

Before delving into how a recursive call appears inside memory, we should understand how memory is divided internally and which parts of the program is stored in which sections of the memory. The memory model discussed here is specific to C language, but the concepts are similar in other popular programming languages as well. The lifecycle of a C language program is as follows:

The compilation and linking of a C language program is out of scope for this book, read any good C language book for that. After compiling and linking, a binary executable gets generated (.exe on windows). When this executable is executing (running) it is called a **process**.

Before the execution of a process begins, the CPU allocates a part of the memory in RAM for that process. This memory is referred to as Process address space. A process uses this space to store information related to the program's execution. Figure 1.1 depicts a high-level view of the Process address space.

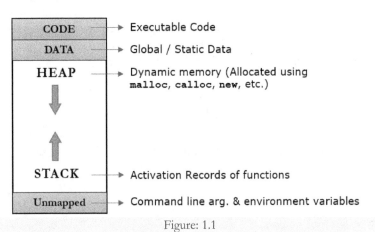

Figure: 1.1

The process address space has following Segments/Areas

1. Code Segment (or Text Area)
2. Data Segment / Data Area
3. Stack Segment / Stack Area

4. Heap Segment / Heap Area

Code segment

✓ This segment contains machine language code (in the form of executable instructions) of the process.

✓ Size of code segment is fixed at load time.

✓ It is a read-only area and does not change during program execution.

✓ This area may be shared across processes so that only a single copy of code is in memory for multiple executing processes[2].

Data Segment

✓ All global and static variables are allocated memory in this segment.

✓ When the program is loading, before execution begins, memory is allocated in this area. As a result, global and static variables are also known as **load-time variables**.

✓ All load-time variables (global and static) are initialized at the load-time before the `main` function is called. If no initial value is given for a variable, it is initialized to the zero of its type[3].

✓ This segment is split into two parts: initialized and uninitialized. When a load-time variable is already initialized in the code, it is allocated memory in the initialized data area; otherwise, it goes into the uninitialized data area. The uninitialized variables are then initialized to zero of their type. The primary reason for storing uninitialized variables separately within the data segment is so that they can all be `memset` to zero using a single operation.

✓ The Size of this segment is also fixed because the number of load-time variables is fixed.

Stack Segment

✓ Stack segment contains **Stack Frames** (also called **Activation Records**) of all the active functions. An active function is currently under the call. It could be running or waiting for the other function to return. Consider the following code in C code example

```
int main(){
    fun1();
}
```

---

[2] Shareable code is outside the scope of this book.

[3] Zero of int data type is 0. Zero of pointer data type is NULL.

```
void fun1(){
   fun2();
}
void fun2(){
}
void fun3(){
   // NEVER CALLED
}
```

`main` function is called first, and it is the only active function at this time. The `main` function calls `fun1`; at this point, `fun1` is executing but both `main` and `fun1` are active, and both of their stack frames are present in the memory's Stack Area. When `fun1` calls `fun2`, execution is in `fun2`, but `main`, `fun1` and `fun2` are all active and have their stack frames in the Stack area.

   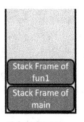 

i) main function called   ii) fun1 function called   iii) fun2 function called   ii) fun2 function returned   ii) fun1 function returned

Memory Stack

When function `fun2` returns, the Stack Frame of `fun2` is popped from the Stack, and execution returns to `fun1`. `main` and `fun1` are currently active with Instruction Pointer in `fun1`. `fun3` is never active because it is never called, and thus its stack frame is never created.

✓ When a function is called, its Stack Frame is created and pushed to the top of the stack.

✓ When a function returns, the corresponding Stack Frame is poped from the Stack.

✓ Size of the Stack Area keeps changing during the execution of the program.

✓ Non-static local variables of a function are allocated memory in Stack Frame of that function when it is active.

✓ Variables allocated memory on Stack are not initialized by default. If initial value of a variable is not specified, it is not initialized, and its value is garbage (this is different from load-time variables allocated memory in the Data Segment).

✓ Stack Frame also contains the information required for the function execution.

✓ Function whose Stack Frame is at top of the Stack is the one that is currently running. Function whose stack frame is in the Stack, but not at the top is active, but its execution is suspended. When all the stack frames above it are popped out, it will resume the execution.

✓ If a function is recursive, multiple stack frames of that function may exist in the Stack at the same time, which implies that there are multiple copies of local non-static variables (one copy in each stack frame). This is unlike the local static variables that are allocated memory only once in the Data Area.

Heap Segment

✓ If you allocate memory at run time using `malloc()`, `calloc()`, or `realloc()` in C language (`new`, or `new[]` in C++), the memory is allocated in the Heap area. Note that in languages like Java, all objects (except for primitive types) are allocated memory in the Heap only.

✓ In C language, there is no way to initialize the memory allocated on Heap. C++, C#, and Java use constructors to initialize object on Heap.

✓ Memory in the Heap area does not have a name (unlike Data and Stack segments). This memory can only be accessed via pointers pointing to it. If we lose the address of this memory (when no pointer points to it), there is no way to access it, and the memory becomes a memory leak. It is one of the most common causes of error in C/C++ programming. The garbage collector in Java automatically frees the heap memory that is not referenced by any object.

✓ In most implementations, both Heap and Stack segment shares a common area and grows toward each other.

Please do not consider this memory model discussion to be the final word. There could be (and probably are) more than four memory areas. They are used to store environment variables or command-line parameters, among other things. The goal here is to provide a simple image to visualize a piece of code in action.

Picture of a running program

When our code (in C language) starts executing, a part of RAM is allocated to it, where the process will be loaded, we have already seen how this memory is divided into multiple areas. **Loading** of a process has following steps:

✓ **Code goes in code area.** Code is in the form of machine language instructions and Instruction Pointer (IP) holds the address of current instruction being executed.

✓ **Global and static variables are allocated memory in the data area.** The data area is divided into two sections: initialized and un-initialized data areas. If we provide the initial value of a variable, it is allocated in the initialized data area; otherwise, memory for the variable is allocated in the un-initialized data area and it is initialized with zero.

✓ **Global and static variables are always initialized.** If initial value is given explicitly, variables are initialized with that value, otherwise they are initialized with zeros of their data types.

```
int x = 5; // initialized with 5
int y;     // initialized with 0
```

> ✓ Code goes in code area
> ✓ Global and static variables are allocated memory in the data area.
> ✓ Global and static variables are initialized.

LOADING

✓ main function is called

After these steps, we say that *the program is now loaded in the memory*. After loading, the main function is called, and the actual execution of the program begins. Read the following code carefully:

```
int total; // Data area. Load time. Initialized to 0.

// When called, its Stack Frame goes in Stack area.
int square(int x){
  // x allocated in stack frame.
  return x*x;
}

// When called, its Stack Frame goes in Stack area.
int squareOfSum(int x, int y){
  static int count = 0; // Load-time. Data Area
  printf("Fun called %d times ", ++count);
  return square(x+y);
}
```

```
int main(){
    int a=4, b=2; //Stack Frame. When function executes
    total = squareOfSum(a, b);
    printf("Square of Sum = %d", total);
}
```

Code: 1.14

This program computes $(a+b)^2$, and prints the result. To keep it simple, it is using fixed values 4 and 2 for a and b respectively. The function squareOfSum also keeps a count of how many times it is called inside the static variable count, and prints this value, every time it is called.

Code 1.14 may not be the best implementation, but it serves our purpose. Read the code again, especially the comments and make sure that you understand everything.

The executable is generated after compilation and linking, and when it runs, it is first loaded into memory (RAM). The main function has not yet been called, and the memory looks like the figure below:

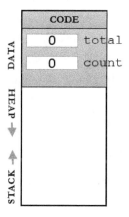

As I previously stated, this is more of a demonstrative figure than an exact representation. After completing the loading, main function is called, and its Stack Frame is created and pushed in the memory Stack. This Stack Frame has

- ✓ Local (non-static) variables of main function (a and b).
- ✓ Other things like the return address.

After `main` function is called, the memory looks like the following:

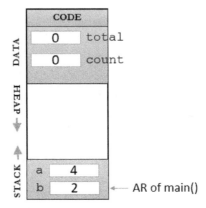

At any time, the point of execution (Instruction Pointer) is inside the function whose Stack frame is at the top of Stack. Let us understand what happens internally when a function is called by another function.

When a function is called:

1. State (register values, Instruction Pointer value, etc.) of calling function is saved in the memory.

2. Stack Frame of the called function is created. Local variables of called function are allocated memory inside this Stack frame.

3. Instruction pointer (IP register) moves to the first executable instruction of called function.

4. Execution of the called function begins.

Similarly, when a function returns to the calling function:

1. Return value of the function is stored in some temporary location.

2. Stack frame of the function is popped from the memory (freed memory gets added to the free pool).

3. State of the previous function is restored back to what it was before the function was called (Point-1 in function call process above).

4. Instruction pointer moves back to the instruction where it was before calling the function and execution begins from the point at which it

was paused[4].

5. Value returned from called function is replaced at the point-of-call in the calling function.

> A function call is an overhead both in terms of time and memory.

One of the reasons behind the popularity of macros in C language (even after all the evil that they bring along) is this overhead in function call[5].

Some compilers optimize the performance by replacing function calls with the entire code of the function during compilation, avoiding the actual function call overhead at run-time. It is known as inline expansion. In Code 1.14, for example, compiler may just put entire code of function `square` inside `squareOfSum` and remove the function call from there.

```
int squareOfSum(int x, int y){
    static int count = 0; // Load-time var
    System.out.print("Fun called "+ ++count +" times");
    return (x+y) * (x+y);
}
```

Code 1.15

Recursive functions are extremely difficult to expand inline, which is another reason why recursion should be avoided wherever possible.

Recursive v/s Non-Recursive inside memory

Let us see what the memory looks like if we miss the terminating condition of recursion and compare it to an infinite loop. Code 1.16, compares the both of them:

```
int main(){            int main(){
    int x = 0;             int x = 0;
    x++;                   x++;
    if(x<5){               while(x<5){
        printf("Hello");       printf("Hello");
```

---

[4] It is conceptually like CPU's **Context Switch** in a single-core muti-processing operating system.

[5] In C++, the inline functions does similar thing.

```
    main();                          }
  }                                  }
}
```

A) Non-terminating recursion   B) Infinite Loop

Code 1.16

In Non-terminated recursion, when `main` function is called for the first time, memory looks like the following diagram. Memory Stack has only one stack frame of function `main`.

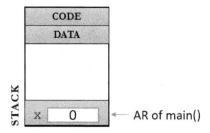

Initial value of x is 0, after increment x become 1. Since x<5, the condition is true and `main` gets called again. A new Stack frame for this newly called `main` function is created in the Memory Stack which is different from the previous `main` function's Stack frame and this also has local variable x that is different from variable x of previous `main` function

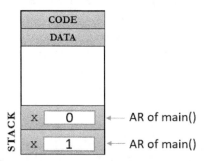

Value of this x in the new function is again 0, and `main` is called again. Every time `main` is called, the value of x in this new function is 0. This is because every instance of `main` is using a different x. The code continues to print "Hello", until there is not more room left in the Stack area to create a new Stack frame. `main` cannot be called any further and the code will crash.

An important thing to note is that "Hello" is not printed indefinitely. It is printed, till the memory stack overflows.

The infinite loop on the other hand has only one function call and hence only one stack frame in the memory. When the execution of this function begins, it will never stop because the condition of while loop never become False. Hence in this case, the program keeps printing "Hello" unless you force-stop it's execution. The memory footprint of this function is not ever-increasing as in the previous case.

Consider Example 1.1 again.

```
int sum(int n){
   if(n == 1)
      return 1;
   else
      return n + sum(n-1);
}
```

When we call this function for n=3, as sum(3); It will call sum(2); which will in-turn call sum(1); At this point, the memory stack has three instances of Stack frames of function sum, each having a local variable n, as shown in the following diagram.

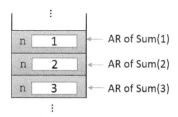

In the iterative version of Example 1.1, there is only one function call to sum(3) and three local variables n, i and sum in the Stack frame of that function.

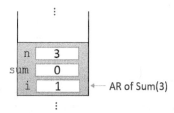

In recursive code, one Stack frame is created for each value of n. If n=1000 then 1000 Stack frames are created. Therefore, the total memory consumed by the recursive function is O(n). while the memory consumption of the iterative function is constant, i.e O(1). Following table gives a comparison of asymptotic running time and memory for recursive and non-recursive sum functions.

	Recursive	Non-Recursive
Time	O(n)	O(n)
Memory	O(n)	O(1)

The asymptotic time taken by the two functions may be same, i.e O(n), but the actual time taken for recursive function is much more than the iterative version because of the time taken to create and destroy all those stack frames.

Example 1.4: Following function is the recursive code to computes factorial of a given number:

```
int factorial(int n){
    if(1==n || 0==n)
        return 1;
    else
        return n * factorial(n-1);
}
```

If factorial function is called for n=4,

fact(4);

to compute factorial of 4. After successive function calls, the memory looks like the following diagram.

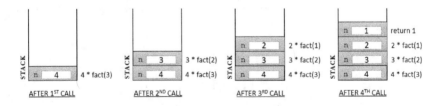

When the functions return, starting from the base case, the corresponding Stack frames are poped from the stack and the stack look like as shown in the following diagram (return value shown on the right side):

36

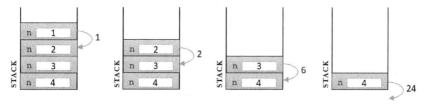

These diagrams do not show the Stack frame of other function in the Memory Stack (eg. `main` function) for the sake of simplicity.

Following is the non-recursive function to compute factorial of n.

```
int factorial(int n) {
    int prod = 1;
    for(int i=0; i<=n; i++)
        prod *= i;
    return prod;
}
```

The memory image of above function is shown in the following diagram.

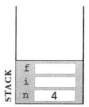

Compare it with the memory taken by the recursive code. This function may have more local variables than the recursive function, but there will always be just one Stack frame.

> Recursion is a huge overhead, both in terms of memory and time. If you have a choice, between writing recursive or non-recursive code, always go for non-recursive.

All the examples of recursion seen till now are simple linear recursions. One of the major problems with recursion comes when recursive calls start overlapping at the sub-problem level. Overlapping subproblems are discussed in the next chapter.

Memory layout as a problem-solving tool

A thorough understanding of a program's lifecycle and how it appears in memory during execution aids in gaining a clear understanding and answering many questions. It is also used to compute the amount of time and memory taken by a function during execution. Consider the following scenarios:

Example 1.5: What will be the value of x in the below C language code?
```
static int x = strlen("Hello");
```

The above code is Compile-time error. To put it simply, *"static and global variables cannot be initialized with the return value of a function"*.

It is trying to initialize a static variable with the return value of function `strlen`. From the previous discussion, we know that static variables are initialized at load time. But wait, functions cannot be called at load time. A function can only be called after loading is complete and the program is executing (first function that gets called is `main`). How can we initialize, at load-time, with something that is not available until execution time. Hence, Error!

What if we break up the statement in two parts?
```
static int x;          // Initialized to zero
x = strlen("Hello");
```

Now there is no problem. At load time variable x is **initialized** to zero. During execution, the function `strlen("Hello")` is called and x is **assigned** the value 5.

Example 1.6: What value will get printed if we call function `fun`?
```
void fun(){
    int a = 5;
    static int b = a;
    printf("Value: %d", b);
}
```

No, the answer is not 5 or 0. The above code is also a compile time ERROR.

We know, static variables are initialized at load time. In above code we are initializing b with a, but variable a, is not available at the time of loading. It will be allocated memory in the Stack frame of `fun`, when function `fun` is called at the time of execution. It is called only after the loading is complete and code starts executing.

Another reason why a static variable cannot be initialized with local non-static variables is that non-static local variables may have multiple copies in the memory when there are more than one instances of a function in the stack frame. Recursive functions have more than one stack frames and each stack frame has a separate copy of all local non-static variables .

Load-time variables cannot be initialized with local variables.

Conclusions

1.   A function has multiple Stack frames inside the memory stack **if and only if** it is recursive.

2.   Global and static variables can only be initialized with constants.

3.   The memory to load-time variables is allocated before any function is called.

4.   The memory allocated to load-time variables is released only after the execution is complete.

We have not discussed the Heap area in detail because the purpose was to explain recursion and not pointers or dynamic memory allocation or deallocation. To learn how heap area is used, read some good book on pointers in C/C++.

2

Jargons of Dynamic Programming

Introduction

Dynamic Programming is associated with a lot of keywords.

- Recursion
- Overlapping subproblems
- Optimal substructure
- Memoization
- Tabulation
- Top-Down vs Bottom-Up Approach of Programming
- Dynamic Programming

Someone did not do a good job choosing these names because the meanings are not obvious. In the previous chapter, we went over recursion in depth. The remaining topics will be covered in this chapter. In this chapter, we try to understand these terms using a simple example of the Fibonacci series. The Fibonacci sequence is shown below,

```
0, 1, 1, 2, 3, 5, 8, 13, 21, ...
```

The sequence begins with zero. The first two terms of the Fibonacci sequence are 0 and 1, and each subsequent term is the sum of the two preceding terms. Recursive definition of Fibonacci number[6] is

```
Fib(n) = Fib(n-1) + Fib(n-2)        if n>2
       = 1                           for n=1
       = 0                           for n=0
```

The simplest algorithm to compute n^{th} term of Fibonacci is direct translation of its mathematical definition:

```
int fib(int n){
  if (n==0)
    return 0
  if (n==1)
    return 1;
  else
    return fib(n-1) + fib(n-2);
}
```

Code: 2.1

Code 2.1 should have an additional check to throw an exception (or handle) when n is negative. We omitted the check to keep the code simple.

Overlapping subproblems

How much time does Code 2.1 take? How can we find the time taken in

---

[6] **Susantha Goonatilake, Toward a Global Science. Mining Civilizational Knowledge, Page 126,** The name of Leonardo of Pisa, also called Fibonacci (1170-1250), is attached with the sequence 0, 1, 1, 2 3, 5, 8, 13, ... , in which the nth term is given by U(N) = U(N-1) + U(N-2). But the sequence was well known in India much before Leonardo's time. Indian authorities on the metrical sciences used this sequence in works on metric. The numbers and the method for their formation is attributed in parts to Pingala (B.C 200), Virahanka (between A.D. 600 and 800), Gopala (prior to A.D. 1135) and Hemacandra (A.D. 1150), all prior to L. Fibonacci (c. A.D. 1202). Narayana Pandita (A.D. 1356) established a relation between his smasika-pankti which contains Fibonacci numbers as a particular case. and "the multinomial coefficients".

this case? Let us start by finding how many times the function is called. The following table list the number of times the function gets called for different values of n.

n	fib(n)	Number of times function is called
2	1	1
3	2	3
4	3	5
6	8	15
7	13	25
9	34	67
10	55	109
15	610	1219
20	6765	13529
25	75025	150049
30	832040	1664079
35	9227465	18454929
40	102334155	204668309

Table 2.1

You can see that the number of function calls are growing exponentially with n. The function calls itself 109 times to compute the 10th term of Fibonacci, and 13529 times to compute the 20th term. The number of calls increases to around 1.6 million for the 30th term, and the function calls itself more than 200 million times to find the 40th term. This function has no complex code, and each instance of the function takes constant time, but because there are so many instances of this function, this seemingly simple code ends up taking exponential time, $O(2^n)$.

Following diagram depicts the function calls for n=5, each node in the diagram represents a function call and value in the node represents value of n in that call.

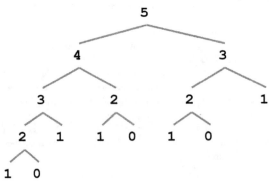

The function `fib(n)`, where n=5, call itself twice, first with n=4 and then with n=3. Function with n=4 will in turn calls itself twice with n=3 and n=2. Note that `fib(3)` is called twice, once from `fib(4)` and `fib(5)` each. Similarly, `fib(2)` is called three times. These function calls will increase like a weed as the value of n increases. Following is the function call tree for n = 7.

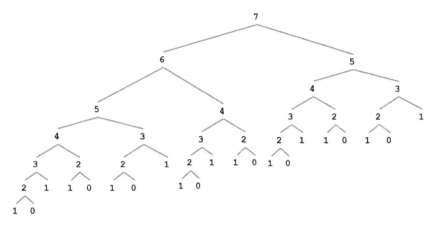

`fib(3)` is called in five times in the above function call tree. It means that we are recomputing the third term of Fibonacci from scratch multiple times. `fib(5)` is computed twice from scratch and `fib(4)` is computed three times from scratch

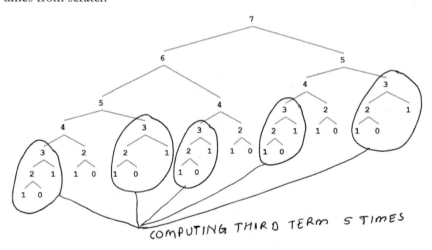

COMPUTING THIRD TERM 5 TIMES

Height of this function call tree is $O(n)$, and it is a balanced binary tree, hence the total number of nodes in this function call tree are $O(2^n)$. Each node of the tree represents a function call, and each function instance takes constant time to execute. As a result, the time complexity of Code 2.1 is

$O(2^n)$, i.e exponential. The equation of time taken by this function is

```
T(n) = T(n-1) + T(n-2) + O(1)
```

You will get the same result if you solve this equation. We rarely use such equations to determine time and memory complexities during interviews or while working in the industry. Most of the time, it is calculated intuitively, as we did, using the function call tree.

The solution of a larger problem in recursion is dependent on the solution of smaller subproblems of the same type. In all the examples of recursion discussed in the first chapter, every subproblems was solved only once. But here when we compute 20th term of Fibonacci using Code 2.1, `fib(3)` is called 2584 times and `fib(10)` is called 89 times. It means that we are computing the 10th term of Fibonacci 89 times, and we solve it from scratch every single time.

In an ideal world, if we have already solved a problem and computed the result, we should use that result instead of solving the same problem again. Despite using recursion, the code would not have been so bad had we only been computing one Fibonacci term only once. Memoization (also known as Top-Down Dynamic programming) is a technique for caching the solution to all subproblems when they are computed for the first time. These pre-computed results are used instead of recomputing the same subproblem when we need to compute it again.

Optimal Substructure

Optimal substructure means that optimal solution of a problem of size n (having n elements) is based on an optimal solution of the same problem of smaller size(s). i.e while building the solution for a problem of size n, split the problem to smaller problems of size, say, k $(k < n)$. We need to find optimal solutions of smaller problem(s) and then combine the solutions to get result of the final solution.

It may not be obvious, but Fibonacci function in Code 2.1 also has optimal substructure property. To find optimal solution for n^{th} term (in this case the correct value of nth term) we need to find the optimal solution (read, correct value) for $(n-1)^{th}$ term and $(n-2)^{th}$ term.

In recursive solution of Fibonacci in Code 2.1, we will get the correct value for n^{th} term only if we have the correct values of $(n-1)^{th}$ and $(n-2)^{th}$ terms. If we are using the same (recursive) function to compute the nth, $(n-1)^{th}$

and $(n-2)$th terms and if that function is correct values for each term, then it means we have an optimal substructure. So loosely speaking, *correct recursion implies Optimal Substructure.*

Example 2.1: Consider finding the shortest route between two cities by car. A user wishes to travel from city A to city C; city B is located between the two. As shown in the following diagram, there are three paths connecting A to B and three paths connecting B to C.

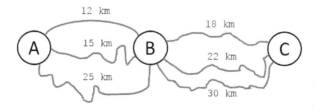

The shortest path of going from A to C (30 km) will involve both, taking the shortest path from A to B as well as the shortest path from B to C. This means:

1. If the shortest route from A to C passes through B, it is the sum of shortest routes from A to B and B to C.

2. If X is a city between A and B and the shortest route from A to C goes through both X and B, the shortest route from A to B will also go through X.

In other words, the problem of going from A to B is nested within the problem of going from A to C.

In a nutshell, this means that we can write recursive solution to the problem of finding the shortest path.

Here the problem of finding the shortest route between two cities demonstrates optimal substructure property. Please note that if you change the problem statement, then it may or may not remain the optimal substructure.

Standard algorithms of Bellman–Ford to find all-pair shortest paths from a single source is a typical example of Dynamic Programming.

Example 2.2: Given four cities, A, B, C and D as well as the distance

45

between them as shown in the following diagram. Find the longest distance from A to D.

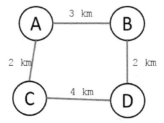

The longest distance from A to D is 6 km, via city C. But this path is not the combination of longest paths from A to C and C to D because the longest path from A to C is 9 km (via B and D).

Clearly longest path problem in this case does not have an optimal substructure property (and hence not a DP problem).

Optimal substructure is Recursion?

In recursive code, the same function is used to solve the main problem as well as all subproblems. In Code 2.1, for example, all Fibonacci terms were computed using the same function. If the function is correct, it should return the correct value for all Fibonacci term.

Is it correct to say that recursion implies Optimal Substructure? In most cases, yes!

Most Algorithms books tell you that Dynamic Programming is applicable to problems with Optimal substructure and overlapping subproblems. I think it will be safe to say, "*If a solution uses recursion and has overlapping subproblems, then that solution can be optimised using recursion*". We'll go over it in more detail later. s

Memoization

We have seen how a recursive solution solves the same subproblem multiple times when it has overlapping subproblems, which can increase the time complexity of code to an exponential level.

Recursion alone is inefficient in terms of execution time and memory usage.

The problem gets even worse when it is coupled with overlapping subproblems. For example, Code 2.1 recalculate value of `fib(x)` from scratch again even if it was previously computed. When `fib(10)` is calculated for the first time we can simply remember the result and store it a cache, so that, next time we want `fib(10)` we can just look into the cache and return the result in `O(1)` time rather than making `109` recursive function calls all over again to compute this value from scratch.

Use of cache along with recursion to avoid solving the same subproblems multiple times is called **Memorization**. Flow chart in Figure 2.1 depicts the execution flow. A subproblem is only solved only if it has never been solved earlier and is then added to the cache.

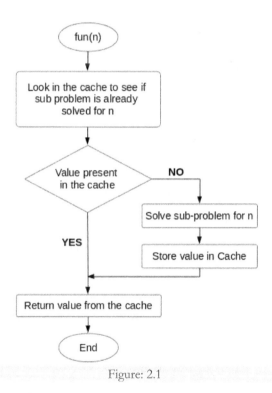

Figure: 2.1

Let us modify Code 2.1 (computing n^th Fibonacci term) to use cache memory. An ideal cache in this case would be a map data structure that allows us to store a <Key, Value> pair, where Key is n and Value is Fibonacci(n). We may also use an integer array, of size N as cache (N = max value of n that need to be computed).

```
int cache[N];
```

The array's elements are all initialized to -1. When k^{th} Fibonacci term is computed for the first time, it is saved in cache[k]. When the function is called again for n=k (to compute k^{th} Fibonacci term), simply return cache[k] in constant time by performing a cache lookup rather than computing it again in O(2^k) time. Following is the modified code:

```
// cache[k]==-1 means fib(k) is not yet computed
int cache[N];
void resetCache(){
  for(int i=0; i<N; i++)
    cache[i] = -1;
}


int fib(int n){
  if(cache[n] == -1){
    if (n==0)
      cache[n] = 0;
    else if (n==1)
      cache[n] = 1;
    else
      cache[n] = fib(n-1)+fib(n-2);
  }
  return cache[n];
}
```

Code: 2.2

In above code, cache array is global. We should discourage the use of global and static variables; This is just for simplicity.

Function fib(n) will only recurse the first time it is called for a value; subsequent calls for that value simply perform a look-up in the cache array and return.

There are two types of calls to the function; those that perform actual computation and thus call the function recursively, and those that simply perform a cache look-up and return the previously computed result. The former is known as non-memoized call and will write into the array, whereas the latter is called memorized call and will only read from the cache array.

Because a location in the cache array is written only once, there are exactly O(n) non-memoized calls. The total time required to compute the nth

Fibonacci term is O(n). Using a simple one-dimensional array as cache reduced an exponential time function to linear time. Compare the function call tree of Code 2.2 to the following function call tree of Code 2.1.

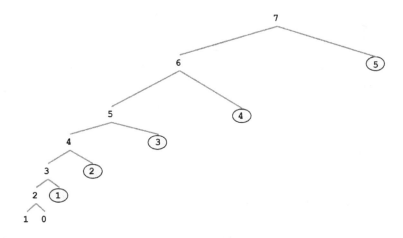

Table 2.2 adds the number of memoization function calls to Table 2.1:

n	fib(n)	Num of times function is called (Recursion)	Num of times function is called (Memoization)
2	1	1	1
3	2	3	3
4	3	5	5
6	8	15	9
7	13	25	11
9	34	67	15
10	55	109	17
15	610	1219	27
20	6765	13529	37
25	75025	150049	47
30	832040	1664079	57
35	9227465	18454929	67
40	102334155	204668309	77

Table: 2.2

For the sake of comparison, if one function call takes one sec to execute[7], Code 2.2 will take just 1.28 minutes to compute the 40th term of Fibonacci,

---

[7] This is a huge-huge extrapolation. A 2 GHz CPU goes through 2,000,000,000 cycles per second.

while the recursive Code 2.1 with Overlapping subproblems will take about 6.5 years to compute the same term. Thankfully we have faster computers that are compensating for our bad code and are doing the work of years in seconds.

> Deciding the Cache is important step in memoization. The cache should be capable of storing results for all the subproblems. Usually, cache is an array or a HashMap. If our problem has only one dimension, then it is one-dim array, else a multi-dimensional

Memoization still use recursion.

Memorization significantly improves performance by avoiding multiple re-computations of the same sub-problem. The simplicity of recursion (the ability to visualise a problem and solve it top-down) combined with the added benefit of no overlapping subproblems makes it a powerful and useful problem-solving technique.

Memoization is recursion without overlapping subproblems. If recursion does not have Overlapping subproblems then Memoization will be same as recursion with an additional cache overhead.

We also know that recursion is bad even without overlapping subproblems and should be avoided. The following Section discusses a non-recursive bottom-up approach to problem solving that reduces both time and space complexity further.

Dynamic Programming

Before moving further, let me add a disclaimer. Just as Apple Inc. bears no resemblance to the fruit 'Apple,' dynamic programming bears no resemblance to being dynamic or even programming. Someone just picked this name to describes a method of problem solving.

Wikipedia defines Dynamic programming as *"A method for solving a complex problem by breaking it down into a collection of simpler subproblems, solving each of those subproblems just once, and storing their solutions - ideally, using a memory-based data structure"*.

By this definition, even Memoization is dynamic programming. Some authors in fact use the term '*Memoized Dynamic Programming*' or '*Top-Down dynamic programming*' for Memoization and they use '*Bottom-up dynamic programming*' or '*Tabulation*' to describe what we are calling Dynamic Programming here.

Dynamic Programming is a non-recursive iterative method of problem solving that demonstrates Optimal Substructure and overlapping subproblems. In other words, if you have a recursive solution with overlapping subproblems, you can use dynamic programming to convert the top-down recursion to bottom-up iteration. As a result, it is essentially a technique for optimising a specific type of recursion.

Developing a Dynamic Programming solution

The logic used in a DP (Dynamic Programming) solution is the same as in the corresponding recursive solution. In recursion, the logic comes naturally, and it is very easy to visualise the solution because it is top-down. The DP solution does not easily to the mind. Most of the time, we write the recursion first and then convert that top-down recursion to bottom-up DP. In most cases, the DP solution save the intermediate results. These intermediate results are usually stored in a memory very similar to the cache used in Memoization. Following code takes the logic from Code 2.1 and the Cache (array) from Code 2.2 and convert the solution from top-down recursion to bottom-up DP.

```
int fib(int n){
  int[] arr = new int[n+1];
  arr[0] = 0;
  arr[1] = 1;
  for(int i=2; i<=n; i++)
    arr[i] = arr[i-1] + arr[i-2];

  return arr[n];
}
```

Code: 2.3

Code 2.3 takes linear time and, it begins with the first term of Fibonacci and keep moving forward (finding the next terms of Fibonacci) until the nth term. It stores the previous terms in array `arr` and use them to compute the next term. In the following section, we will argue whether or not we should save all of the terms.

As you may have noticed, the direction of problem solving in DP is opposite to that of recursion or memorization. Dynamic programming unrolls the solution of recursion and move in opposite direction.

> Both Memoization and Dynamic Programming fix the problem of overlapping sub-problem by solving a subproblem only once.
>
> Memoization uses recursion and work in Top-down recursive way, while Dynamic Programming moves in different direction by solving the problem bottom-up.

Converting recursion to DP

DP is also known as tabulation because in most DP problems, the intermediate results are stored in a table (an array). As discussed earlier the table(array) of DP is same as the cache of Memoization. The only difference is in the way we are visualizing the logic to populate the table. The direction of visualization of logic is opposite in DP (bottom-up vs top-down), but the logic used to populate the table is the same. We should think of DP as a way to optimize recursion, it means that the first step to solve a DP problem is usually to solve it recursively and then extract the logic from that recursion. Once we have a recursive solution, we can either memorize it or can go to the DP solution directly. We will elaborate on this strategy more in the following chapter.

Optimized Dynamic Programming

Having the DP solution does not imply that there is no room for improvement. As the saying goes, the biggest room in life is the room for improvement.

Code 2.3 stores all previous Fibonacci terms. We do not require all of them. At any point, we only need to know the previous two terms to find the next term. The following use only two variables instead of an array.

```
int fib(int n){
  if(n == 0){ return 0; }
  if(n == 1){ return 1; }

  int a = 1; // For (k-2)'th term
  int b = 1; // For (k-1)'th term
  int c;     // For k'th term
```

```
for (int i = 3; i <= n; i++) {
  c = a + b;
  a = b;
  b = c;
}
return c;
}
```

Code 2.4

This section on further optimizing the Dynamic Programming solution is optional and is included only for completion. Not all the DP solutions may have such scope of improvement. The goal is to always leave the possibility of further optimizing a solution open.

Let us compare the four solutions seen in this chapter for finding the nth term of Fibonacci.

Recursion	Memoization	Dynamic Programming	Optimized DP
Use Recursion	Use Recursion	Do not use Recursion	Do not use Recursion
Overlapping subproblems	No Overlapping subproblems	No Overlapping subproblems	No Overlapping subproblems
Top-Down	Top-Down	Bottom-Up	Bottom-Up

Top-Down v/s Bottom-Up

Recursion is a top-down way of problem solving. Memoization is an improvement over recursion when there are overlapping subproblems and Dynamic programming is bottom-up alternative to both, recursion and memoization. Let us look at an example to understand difference between top-down and bottom-up problem solving.

Example 2.3: below is the code to compute factorial of n.

```
int factorial(int n) {
  if(1==n)
    return 1;
  else
    return n * factorial(n-1);
}
```

While defining the solution we have a top-down view. We define factorial(n) in terms of factorial(n-1) and then put a terminating condition at the bottom.

Following diagram shows all the function calls for factorial(4). This is a top-down approach of problem solving. Here, we begin computing the problem with factorial(4), and compute the sub elements as needed to generate the solution.

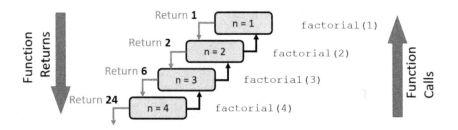

A bottom-up approach on the other hand develops the solution starting from the base case(s).

$$1! = 1$$
$$2! = 2 (1!) = 1$$
$$3! = 3 (2!) = 6$$
$$4! = 4 (3!) = 24$$

In top-down problem-solving, we understand the final destination at the beginning itself and we develop the means required to reach there. On the other hand, bottom-up has all the means available and we keep moving forward till we reach the destination, but the picture of the destination may not be clear in the beginning. Below is an interesting analogy:

Top-down: *You say, "I will take over the world". How will you do that? You say, 'will take over Asia first'. How will you do that? "I will take over India first". How will you do that? "I will first become the Chief Minister of Delhi", etc. etc.*

Bottom-up: *You decide to become the CM of Delhi. After becoming the CM, you work toward taking over India, then all other countries in Asia and finally take over the whole world.*

No matter, how similar it looks, it has nothing to do with any Chief Minister :). Oh! you need an a-political analogy. Let us try the following.

You have a 200 sq. yards empty land on which you want to build a house. There are two approaches.

Top-down: *Draw and finalize the floor-plan and layout on paper. Start building the foundation, pillars and walls, etc.*

Bottom-up: *Start laying down the foundation and building the walls. Start building one room at a time.*

Both the above approaches may result in the construction of the exact same house. But which way of constructing a house, do you think is easier? Top-down is usually more intuitive because we get a bird's eye view, and the broader understanding is clear at the beginning. That's why we start with recursion.

It is worth noting that the first task completed in both Top-down and Bottom-up approaches is Acquiring-Delhi (or building the foundation). Similarly, no matter which approach is used, `factorial(1)` will be computed first. The Top-down approach, has a backlog of computing all the factorials while computing `factorial(1)` (inside Memory Stack in the form of Stack frames).

Binary tree algorithms are the most basic example of a Top-down approach. Following is the pre-order traversal algorithm for a Binary tree:

PreOrder(Root)
    Print data at root
    Traverse left sub-tree in **PreOrder**
    Traverse right sub-tree in **PreOrder**

This algorithm starts from the top and moves toward leaves. Most of the Binary tree algorithms are like this. We start from the top, traverse the tree in some order and keep making the decisions on our way. Consider the below example:

Example 2.4: For each subtree of a given binary tree, add the sum of all the nodes in that subtree to its root node. Following diagram shows a sample input and output.

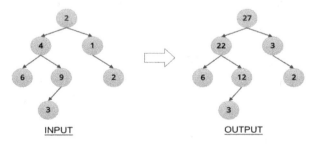

INPUT   OUTPUT

Node with value 9 has only one child, the values of that child get added to 9 and it becomes 12. Node with value 4 has three nodes under it (6, 9 and 3), all these values are added to this node and its final value becomes 22. Similarly, all nodes, except for leaf nodes, have their values updated.

Note: *this problem is not related to DP.*

We do not solve the entire problem in most Binary Tree questions. Only solve the problem for the root node and leave the solution of the left and right sub trees to recursion (each instance of recursion has a different root). We must ensure that our function works for all possible values of root. Following are the five possibilities for a root node:

1. root is null.
2. Both left child and right child of root are null.
3. Left child of root is null, but the right child is not null.
4. Right child of root is null, but the left child is not null.
5. Neither left child, nor right child is null.

If root is null then don't do anything, this could be a terminating condition. Similarly, nothing needs to be done if root is a leaf node, and, this may be the second terminating condition. For rest of the nodes, following is the core logic,

addChildSum(Root)

    addChildSum for Left sub-tree

    addChildSum for Right sub-tree

    Add value of left and Right child nodes to root

Following Code translates the above logic into code.

```
void addChildSum(Node root){
    if(root == null) return; // Terminating cond.

    addChildSum(root.left);   //Compute Left Sub Tree
    addChildSum(root.right); //Compute Right Sub Tree

    if(root.left != NULL)
       root.data += root.left.data;

    If(root.right != NULL)
       Root.data += root.right.data;
```

}

Nothing will change for the leaf nodes. Note that, even when the logic is top-down, the flow of data is always bottom-up.

 INTERVIEW TIP

Recursion *is a top-down approach of problem solving.*

Memoization *is also top-down, but it is an improvement over recursion. It caches the results when a sub-problem is solved and use that result when same sub-problem is encountered again instead of recomputing it. It comes with some drawbacks of recursion, but a problem is solved only once.*

Dynamic programming *attempts to solve the entire problem bottom-up avoiding the recursion altogether.*

Although top-down is easier to understand, bottom-up performance is almost always superior. However, for the sake of completeness, consider one use case in which top-down beats bottom-up.

When to avoid using bottom-up

In most cases, Bottom-up dynamic programming solves all subproblems before solving the main problem. In a top-down approach (recursion or memorised), we solve only the problems that are required to solve the main problem.

As a result, the bottom-up dynamic programming approach may require us to solve more subproblems than necessary. To avoid this, the DP solutions should be properly framed. Consider the following example:

Example 2.5: In combinatorics, Combination is defined recursively:

```
C(n,m) = C(n-1,m) + C(n-1,m-1)
```

Code 7.4 defines a function that take two arguments n and m and return C(n,m). The recursive function to compute this is straight forward:

```
int comb(int n, int m){
    if( n == 0 || m == 0 || n == m )
        return 1;
    else
        return comb(n-1, m) + comb(n-1, m-1);
}
```

The DP solution of this problem requires to construct the entire pascal triangle and return the $(m+1)$th value in the $(n+1)$th row. Row number and column number starts from $(0,0)$. For example, $C(5,4)$ will return the highlighted value in below triangle:

```
            1
         1     1
      1     2     1
   1     3     3     1
 1     4     6     4     1
1     5    10    10     5     1
```

The DP solution will construct the whole triangle and return this value. The recursive solution on the other hand will be computing only the required nodes of pascal triangle as highlighted below

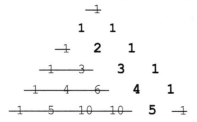

If n and m are very large, recursion may actually outperform DP in terms of both time and memory.

This is just to complete the discussions, otherwise, if dynamic programming can be used, do so, it will almost never disappoint you.

We now understand everything there is to know about Dynamic Programming. The following chapter focuses on the strategy for solving any dynamic programming problem asked in coding competitions or during interviews. Before proceeding to the next chapter, consider the following concepts that are used in some DP problems.

Subarray, subsequence and subset

This section is not directly related to dynamic programming, but these three terms are used in lot of problems related to arrays, strings and linked list. It is important to understand these terms because most DP problems also use array datastructure.

Subarray

A subarray of an array is a continuous section of the array with the same relative order of elements as the original array. If $\{1,2,3,4,5\}$ is the original array then $\{2,3,4\}$ is one of the subarrays but $\{2,4\}$ and $\{3,2\}$ are not because $\{2,4\}$ is not continuous chunk of the array and the order of elements in $\{3,2\}$ is not the same as that in the original array. An array of size n has a total of $\dfrac{n(n+1)}{2}$ subarrays.

To print all subarrays of a given array using brute-force logic, use two nested loops as shown below.

```
void printSubarrays(int[] a){
  for(int i=0; i<a.length; i++){
    for(int j=i; j<a.length; j++){
      printArray(a, i, j);
    }
  }
}
```

Code: 2.5

The printArray function is called once for each subarray. The brute-force cost of finding all the subarrays is $O(n^2)$ and Code 2.5 takes $O(n^3)$ time that also include the time to print each subarray.

Subsequence

A Subsequence maintains the relative order of elements from the original array but the elements may not be contiguous part of the array itself. For example, if $\{1, 2, 3, 4, 5\}$ is the array then $\{1, 2, 4\}$ is one of the subsequences, but $\{3, 2\}$ is not because the elements are not in the same order. Total number of subsequences of an array of size n are $2^n - 1$.

We can use the include-exclude logic to get all the subsequences of an array (or list). We have two options for each element of the array,

1. Include it in the subsequence.
2. Does not include (Exculde) the element from the current subsequence.

The following code print all the subsequences of the given array. The approach is same, for every element in the array, there are two choices, either to include it in the subsequence or not to include it. We apply this for every element in the array starting from the first elemtn, until we reach the last index. Once the last index is reached, the current subsequence is either printed (or added to the list of already computed subsequences depending on the question).

```java
void printSubseq(int[] arr, int idx,
                            ArrayList<Integer> path) {
  // TERMINATING CONDITION
  if (idx == arr.length) {
    System.out.println(path);
    return;
  }

  // EXCLUDING THE CURRENT ELEMENT
  printSubsequences(arr, idx + 1, path);

  // INCLUDING THE CURRENT ELEMENT
  path.add(arr[idx]);
  printSubsequences(arr, idx + 1, path);

  path.remove(path.size() - 1);
}
```

Code: 2.6

This is a recursive function that takes $O(2^n)$ time and $O(n)$ extra memory. If the given array is {1, 2, 3}, then following function call tree represents the above recursion:

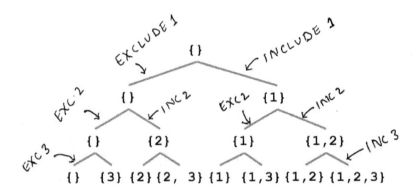

The left side of a node is the recursion for Ecluding the current element and right side for including the element. The height of this function call tree is $O(n)$, and number of nodes are $O(2^n)$. The logic in Code 6.4 is very similar to finding all root-to-leaf paths in a binary tree.

Subset

In a set, the ordering of elements is not important hence the relative order of elements may not be the same and they may not be contiguous part of the original array. So a subset can be any permutation of the subsequence.

3

Strategy for DP Problems

Most people consider DP problems to be one of the most difficult types of interview questions. We will try to devise a strategy that can be used to start solving, if not completely solve, any DP problem. Before developing a methodical approach, consider the following interesting facts related to Dynamic Programming and the conclusions drawn from them.

1. DP is an optimization of the recursion. Try to find the recursive solution first before even thinking about DP. This is THE most crucial point. Many people try to remember the DP solution directly without understanding the recursion. If you do this, you will have a memorize every single DP problem.

2. A recursive solution, no matter how bad it is, is a working solution that demonstrates your problem-solving skills. Many interviewers may even accept the recursive solution as the final solution.

3. The logic of DP comes from recursion. DP just apply the same logic in a different direction.

4. The array/list/table used in DP is same as the cache used in Memoization. If you can figure out the data structure yourself, you can

skip this intermediate step of Memoization.

We can conclude from the preceding points that obtaining the correct recursive solution is the first and most important step in Dynamic Programming. The logic of DP is derived directly from recursion, and even when we are unable to provide the final DP solution, a recursive solution is a working solution. Providing a working solution is important during the interview, even if getting the best solution is the best thing.

Use the following steps as template to solve any DP problem.

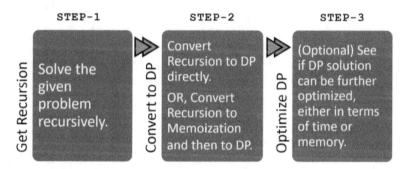

Figure 3.1: Steps to solving a DP Problem

Both Memoization and DP rely on Recursion logic. These methods have already been discussed in previous chapters. Interestingly, memoization and DP take same asymptotic time and space in most problems. Obviously, DP is the best, but the difference between DP and Memoization is in terms of constant multiplier. In next sections we are just revising these three concepts with the help of an example.

Get Recursion

Most of the time, when you see a problem, you have no idea that it is a DP problem. Only after you have found the recursive solution should you think about optimizing it further with DP. The first chapter discussed developing recursive solutions.

✓ Define the work performed by each function.
✓ Define the work that will be delegated to the recursive function calls.
✓ Define one or more terminating conditions.

Consider the following example:

Example 3.1: Given a two-dimensional array of order M*N. Given that we can only move forward or rightward, what is the total number of ways in which we can move from the top-left cell (arr[0][0]) to the bottom-right cell (arr[M-1][N-1])? There are two ways to get to the bottom-right cell in a 2*2 matrix. There are six ways to get from the top-left corner to the bottom-right corner of a 3*3 matrix. As shown in the diagram below, there are three ways to go from cell (0,0) to cell (1, 2) in a 2*3 array.

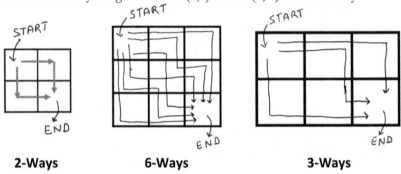

| **2-Ways** | **6-Ways** | **3-Ways** |

Chapter 4 discusses the DP problem related to finding the path in detail.

What is the recursion for this problem? One of the key points in recursion is, **"Do not solve the entire problem"**, instead, **"Define the larger solution in terms of smaller solutions of the same type"**. Another important thing is the way you define and read the signature of the function. In this problem, we want to count the number of ways to reach a cell from (0,0), let the signature of the function be the following,

```
int numOfWays(int m, int n)
```

This function will, *Find the number of ways in which we can reach cell (m,n) from cell (0,0)*. The way we read the signature is very important in understanding recursion.

We have taken only the destination cell as variable. The source cell, i.e (0,0) is fixed and not passed as parameter to the function. The way you define the solution will change if you also take source as parameter. We categorize the DP solutions based on number of parameters in Chapter 5.

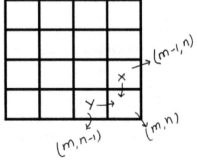

Just before reaching (m,n), we are either in cell $(m-1,n)$ or $(m,n-1)$. Let us assume that there are x ways of reaching cell $(m-1,n)$ and y ways in which we can reach $(m,n-1)$. Then in x different ways we can come to (m,n) from the top and in y different ways we can come to (m,n) from the left side. So total number of ways of reaching (m,n) are x+y. In a nutshell, the Number of ways to reach cell (m,n) is a sum of number of ways of reaching cell $(m-1,n)$ and number of ways of reaching $(m,n-1)$.

```
numOfWays(m,n) = numOfWays(m-1,n) + numOfWays(m,n-1)
```

We have the recursion; all that remains is to add the terminating condition. There is only one way to reach any cell in the first row or first column, except for the top-left corner cell, i.e the starting point. Following code is the recursive solution to the given problem:

```
int numOfWays(int m, int n){
    if(m == 0 && n == 0) // IF AT START
        return 0;
    if(m == 0 || n == 0) // IF IN 1st ROW or 1st COL
        return 1;

    int x = numOfWays(m-1, n);
    int y = numOfWays(m, n-1);
    return x+y;
}
```

Code 3.1

This code is an exponential-time recursive solution that demonstrates Optimal substructure and overlapping subproblems. We can use the following function call tree to demonstrate that the time complexity is exponential. Following diagram is the function calls for a 4x4 matrix.

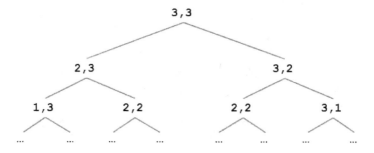

The function is first called for the bottom-right cell, i.e $(3, 3)$, and then every function calls itself twice. Height of this function call tree is $O(n)$, for an array of order $n*n$, and each node of this tree represents a function call which takes constant time. Being a balanced binary tree, total number of nodes are $O(2^n)$. Hence, the total time taken is also $O(2^n)$, exponential. Same function call tree can be used to prove that the recursion takes $O(n)$ memory (equal to the height of the tree).

As a rule of thumb, if a function calls itself twice recursive and the parameters are reduced by one in each call, the time taken by the function is $O(2^n)$. This rule can also be extrapolated to more than two recursive function calls.

Optimal substructure: Because we are using recursion, it is enough to state that the solution has Optimal substructure. But here's another way to look at it.

- **Larger Problem**: Determine number of ways to reach cell (3,3).
- **Smaller Problem-1**: Determine number of ways to reach cell (2,3).
- **Smaller Problem-2**: Determine number of ways to reach cell (3,2).

We should have optimal solutions to smaller problems in order to have optimal solutions to larger problem, hence optimal substructure.

Overlapping subproblems: The number of ways to reach cell (2,2) is computed twice in the function call tree of a 4*4 matrix. The larger problem is solving the exact same smaller subproblem more than once.

As a result, the solution includes both optimal substructure and overlapping subproblems. This is a good candidate for Dynamic Programming.

Convert Recursion to DP

1. Recursion to Memoization

What kind of cache should we use? In this problem, we want to keep track of the number of ways of reaching a cell from (0,0). We can use a two-dimensional array of same size as the given array and store the numOfWays(i,j) in cache[i][j]. Assume there is a global 2-dim array cache[8] with each element initialized to -1.

```
int numOfWays(int m, int n){
  if(cache[m][n] != -1)
    return cache[m][n];

  if(m == 0 && n == 0) // IF WE ARE AT START
    cache[m][n] = 0;
  if(m == 0 || n == 0) // IF IN 1st ROW or 1st COL
    cache[m][n] = 1;
  else
    cache[m][n] = numOfWays(m-1, n)+numOfWays(m, n-1);

  return cache[m][n];
}
```

Code 3.2

If number of ways of reaching cell (m,n) has already been computed, use the previously computed value without recomputing it again, otherwise compute the value and store it in the cache for later use.

This is called memorization. How much time does this code take? In this case, how can we compute the time complexity intuitively? We could draw the function call diagram as well, but there is an even easier way to determine how long this function takes. There are M*N cells in cache. We only write to each cell once and read from it twice (the value of cache[i][j] is read to populate cache[i+1][j] and cache[i][j+1] only). Three operations per cell imply constant time per cell, so the total time taken is O(m*n).

Memoization and Dynamic Programming have the same asymptotic time complexity in most cases.

2. Recursion to Dynamic Programming

The bottom-up DP solution takes the logic from recursion and cache from memorization and populate that table in the opposite direction. Follow the following steps to construct the DP solution,

---

[8] This is just for example; otherwise global and static variables should be discouraged.

✓ Use logic from recursion.
✓ Use a temporary memory similar to the cache of memoization.
✓ Apply the logic of recursion in opposite direction (to that of recursion).
✓ Because the direction of application of logic is opposite, the terminating condition in recursion becomes the Initialization in DP.

Following diagram has the recursive and DP solutions of Fibonacci seen in the Chapter 2.

RECURSION

Terminating Cond. Becomes Initialization

```
int fib(int n){
   if (n==0)
      return 0;
   if (n==1)
      return 1;
   else
      return fib(n-1) + fib(n-2);
}
```

DYNAMIC PROGRAMMING

→ Same as memoization

```
int fib(int n){
   int arr[100];
   arr[0] = 0;
   arr[1] = 1;
   for(int i=2; i<=n; i++)
      arr[i] = arr[i-1]+arr[i-2];
   return arr[n];
}
```

· Logic remains same
· Direction of Logic is opposite.

Use the above approach to relook at code 3.1 as shown below.

```
int numOfWays(int m, int n){
   if(m == 0 && n == 0)
      return 0;
   if(m == 0 || n == 0)
      return 1;

   return numOfWays(m-1, n) + numOfWays(m, n-1);
}
```

Terminating Conditions

LOGIC: ADD VALUES OF TOP & LEFT CELLS

DIRECTION: START FROM BOTTOM - RIGHT CELL.

Now let us use the logic of recursive solution (Code 3.1) and cache of Memoization (Code 3.2) to form the Dynamic Programming solution of the given problem.

i) Use the right tabulation.

In this case, the matrix is a two-dimensional array because that is what we used as cache during memorization. With some practise, you'll be able to determine the type of array to use in a DP solution, and you'll be able to skip memoization. In most cases, use a 2-dim array in when solution contains two variables.

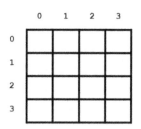

In DP solution, we should think about populating this array from the top-left which is the opposite direction from recursion.

ii) Convert Terminating condition of recursion to initialization.

```
// IF m&n are both 0s then we return 0
arr[0][0] = 0;
```

```
// THERE IS ONLY 1 WAY TO GO TO
// ANY CELL IN 1st ROW or 1st COL
for(int i=1; i<m; i++)
    arr[i][0] = 1;
for(int i=1; i<n; i++)
    arr[0][i] = 1;
```

	0	1	2	3
0	0	1	1	1
1	1			
2	1			
3	1			

After initialising the first row and first column (as per the terminating conditions of recursion), populate the rest of the matrix using the core logic of recursion.

iii) Use logic of recursion in opposite direction to populate the table.

Populate the matrix top-down using the exact same logic of recursion.

```
for(int i=1; i<m; i++)
    for(int j=1; j<n; j++)
        arr[i][j] = a[i-1][j]+a[i][j-1];
```

The final value of cell (i,j) represents the number of ways of going from cell (0,0) to cell (i,j).

	0	1	2	3
0	0	1	1	1
1	1	2	3	4
2	1	3	6	10
3	1	4	10	20

Following is the complete DP solution of the problem.

```
int numOfWays(int m, int n){
    int arr[m][n];
```

```
arr[0][0] = 0;
for(int i=1; i< m; i++)
   arr[i][0] = 1;
for(int i=1; i< n; i++)
   arr[0][i] = 1;

for(int i=1; i<m; i++)
   for(int j=1; j<n; j++)
      arr[i][j] = a[i-1][j] + a[i][j-1];

return arr[m-1][n-1];
}
```

Code 3.3

Code 3.3 consumes $O(m*n)$ time and $O(m*n)$ extra memory. Although time is asymptotically equal memorization, the DP solution's total time is significantly less because it does not use any recursion.

Optimize DP

\
If I were the interviewer, I would probably ask, "Can this solution be further optimised?".

Even if further optimization is not possible, this is one way to test how confident a good candidate is in his solution. Interviews are not interrogations, but rather discussions; this is also a way of starting an advance discussion even if I, as an interviewer, does not know the solution.

Here comes the question; Can we further optimize Code 3.3?

Yes, the answer is yes!

At least we can reduce the amount of extra memory we use. Code 3.3 allocates $O(m.n)$ extra memory. To find the values of cells in a row, we only need the previous row (and not the rows before that). So, we can manage with two one-dimensional arrays of size n instead of using a 2-dim array of size m*n.

Use two arrays representing the previous row and the current row. Use values in the previous row to populate the current row. Then, the current row becomes the previous row whose values will be used to populate the next row. This way, the total memory used will be 2n.

 INTERVIEW TIP

Code 3.1 is a working solution. It is taking exponential time or more time than the optimal solution, but it is syntactically, semantically, and logically correct..

In many cases, especially if you are being interviewed for an Engineering Manager profile where coding is not the primary expectation, it may be sufficient to solve the problem up to this point. However then also, please engage in the discussion and inform the interviewer that it may not be the most optimal solution and you can further optimise it using DP.

Coming up with memoization solution for a problem is much easier than standard iterative DP solution. If you find the conversion to DP challenging, consider memoization. It has a running time, that is asymptotically same as the optimal solution.

 COMPETITIVE CODING TIP

In a coding competition (Online or otherwise) the recursive solution may not be sufficient. Some of the test cases in an online competition may fail due to the long execution time of the recursive code (even when the result is correct). Also, during the competition, your code will be compared to the code of the other competitors.

Consider one more example to see the above strategy in action.

Example 3.2: A route has N stations, from 0 to N-1. A train travels only forward from the first station (Station 0) to the last station (Station N-1). If the cost of a ticket between any two stations is given, calculate the cheapest way to travel from station 0 to station N-1. For example, let there be 4 stations, and the cost of travel between them is given in a 4*4 matrix, where cost[i][j] is the cost of a ticket from station i to station j.

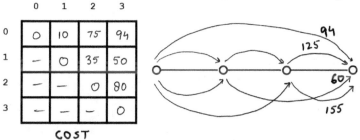

COST

Since there is no moving backward, cost[i][j] does not make any sense when i>j, and hence they are all left blank. If i==j, the cost of travel is zero. You may think of using a sparse array for this cost matrix.

Following are the two ways to go to `station-2`

i)   Go directly from 0 to 2. A direct ticket from `station-0` to `station-2` costs 75.

ii)   First go from `station-0` to `station-1`, then go to `station-2` from `station-1`. This way total cost of travel is 45 (10+35).

In the given example there are 4 stations, and we need to find the minimum cost of travel from `station-0` to `station-3`. There are four different ways of reaching `station-3` and the most optimal way of travel is to go from `Station-0` to `Station-1` and then directly from `Station-1` to `Station-3`. I can think of at least two ways of defining the solution, resulting in two different function signatures.

i)   Find the cheapest way to go from a source to a destination. There are two variables here, source and destination.
      `int getMinCost(int s, int d)`

ii)   Find the cheapest way to reach a destination. There is only one variable here, i.e destination. The source is assumed to be `Station-0`.
      `int getMinCost(int d)`

The first DP solution should probably use a 2-dim array because there are two variables, and the second DP solution should most likely use a 1-dim array. We'll get to it later; first, let's get the recursion right.

Function `minCost(s, d)` returns the minimum cost to travel from `station-s` to `station-d`. There are two ways in which we can go from `station-s` to `station-d`.

i)   Go directly from s to d.
ii)   Take at least one break in going from s to d. This break can be at any station between s and d (i.e from s+1 to d-1).

There is only one way of directly going from s to d, but there are so many ways in which a person can take breaks, we should explore all the possibilities. Essentially, we should explore all possibilities where a person can be just before reaching the destination. This approach is discussed in detail in the next chapter.

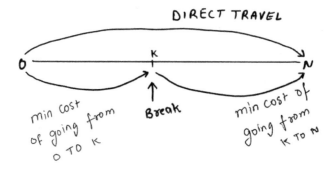

DIRECT TRAVEL

When a person takes a break at any station k (0<k<N), it may not be the only break, he may (or may not) take more breaks between 0-k and k-N. The Minimum cost of going from 0 to N-1 is the minimum out of all of these options and can be recursively defined as

```
minCost(0, N-1)
      = MIN { cost[0][n-1],
              cost[0][1] + minCost(1, N-1),
              minCost(0, 2) + minCost(2, N-1),
              ... ... ...,
              minCost(0, N-2) + cost[N-2][n-1] }
```

where cost[i][j] is the direct cost of travel from i to j which comes from the cost matrix, and minCost(i,j) is minimum cost of travel that may include breaks. The later can be computed by calling the same function recursively. Following may be the terminating conditions for this recursion:

```
// 1. WHEN BOTH STATIONS ARE SAME.
IF(s == d) RETURN 0.

// 2. WHEN s IS JUST BEFORE d, THERE IS ONLY 1 WAY
IF(s == d-1) RETURN cost[s][d].
```

Both the preceding conditions can be combined into one.

```
IF (s <= d) return cost[s][d].
```

Following is the complete recursive solution for the given problem assuming that the cost matrix is global:

```
// Calculate min cost from source(s) to destination(d)
int getMinCost(int s, int d){
   if (s == d || s == d-1)
      return cost[s][d];
```

```
int minCost = cost[s][d];
for (int i = s+1; i<d; i++){
  // Minimum cost of going from s to i
  // and then minCost from i to d.
  int temp = getMinCost(s, i) + getMinCost(i, d);
  if (temp < minCost)
    minCost = temp;
}
return minCost;
}
```

Code: 3.4

Code 3.4 demonstrates optimal substructure property because we compute the minimum cost of travel between intermediate stations to find the minimum price of going from the initial source to the final destination.

The code solves same subproblems multiple times. For example, to find the minimum cost from station-0 to station-4, we compute minimum cost from station-1 to station-3 twice, as shown in the following diagram.

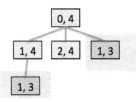

You might have guessed that Code 3.4 takes exponential time. The height of the function call tree is O(n), and each node has O(n) children, so the total time taken is $O(n^n)$, i.e exponential.

Code 3.4 can be memoized in the similar manner using a 2-dim array of size N*N as a cache that stores the minimum cost of travel between two corresponding stations. When the minimum cost of travel from station-s to station-d is computed, it is stored in cell cache[s][d]. Following is the memorized code that uses a cache memory.

```
int getMinCost(int s, int d){
  if (s == d || s == d-1)
    return cost[s][d]; // Direct cost of s to d
```

```
if(cache[s][d] == 0){ // Not yet computed
  // Code Similar to recursive version
  int minCost = cost[s][d];

  for (int i = s+1; i<d; i++){
    int temp = getMinCost(s, i) + getMinCost(i,d);
    if (temp < minCost)
      minCost = temp;
  }
  cache[s][d] = minCost; // Add minCost to cache
}
return caches[s][d];
}
```

Code: 3.5

Deciding the Cache is the most important step in memoization. It should be capable of storing results of all the subproblems with a constant look-up time. In most problems, cache is an array.

Code 3.5 vastly improves on Code 3.4's exponential-time recursive solution. Before converting this recursion to DP, let us also discuss the second approach where we accept only the destination as parameter and assume the source to be Station-0. This function should compute and return the minimum cost of travel to Station-n. The signature of that function is,

`int getMinCost(int n)`

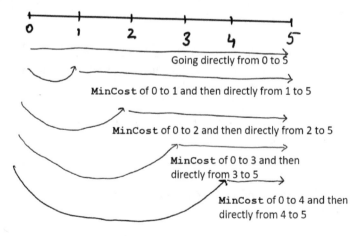

In the previous diagram whenever we compute minCost, the source is always 0. The main problem of going to Station-n is defined in terms of multiple subproblems of going to Station-k where (0<k<n). Following is the code for a fixed source. It also assumes that the cost matrix is global.:

```
// Calculate min cost from 0 to n
int getMinCost(int n){
    if (n == 0 || n == 1)
        return cost[0][n];

    int minCost = cost[0][n]; // DIRECT COST
    for (int i = 1; i<n; i++){
        // Minimum cost of going from 0 to i
        // and then direct cost from i to n.
        int temp = getMinCost(i) + cost[i][n];
        if (temp < minCost)
            minCost = temp;
    }
    return minCost;
}
```

Code: 3.6

Code 3.6 takes less time than Code 3.4, even though both takes exponential time and has overlapping subproblems.

Code 3.6 can be memorized using a one-dimensional array as the cache. When minimum cost to reach Station-k is computed for the first time, store it in cache[k].

Let us directly convert the recursion in Code 3.6 to Dynamic Programming. The DP solution should use a 1-dim array and populate it in opposite direction (i.e from the beginning of the array).

First, initialize the array according to the terminating condition of recursion.

```
arr[0] = cost[0][0];
arr[1] = cost[0][1];
```

These two elements represent the minimum cost of reaching Station-0 and Station-1.

Now, use the core logic of recursion from Code 3.6, and find the minimum cost of reaching all station, starting from Station-2 and keep adding that value to this array. Following is the complete DP solution.

```
int getMinCost(int n){
  int[] arr = new int[n+1]; // ARRAY TO STORE MinCost
  arr[0] = cost[0][0];
  arr[1] = cost[0][1];

  for (int k = 2; k<=n; k++){
    // Minimum cost of going from 0 to k
    int minCost = cost[0][k];
    for(int i=1; i<k; i++){
      int temp = arr[i] + cost[i][k];
      if (temp < minCost)
        minCost = temp;
    }
    arr[k] = minCost;
  }
  return arr[n];
}
```

Code: 3.7

Pre-computed minimum cost of travel to station x, where (0<x<k), stored in array arr are used to find the minimum cost of travel to station-k.

I believe we have the steps to solving dynamic programming problems nailed down. In the following section, we will go over another important strategy for solving DP problems.

Use Recursion to Map similar DP problems.

Consider the following example to better understand this strategy.

Example 3.3: Determine the unique number of ways a rectangular plot of dimension 2*n can be tiled with bricks of dimension 2 x 1 each. A brick can only be placed vertically or horizontally. For example, one of the ways of tiling a plot of length n = 5 is shown in the following figure.

The function should return the total number of unique ways in which we can place the bricks.

 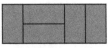

Empty plot   **Tiled with Bricks**

Recursion

For Recursion, we must first define the function's signature (or the problem statement). The task is to determine the number of different ways bricks can be placed to tile a plot of length n and width 2. Following is the signature of function that finds the number of ways,

```
int numOfWays(int n)
```

Now that we have the signature, let us attempt to place our first brick. The first brick can be placed either horizontally or vertically.

1. If we place the first brick vertically, the problem is reduced to finding:
    Number of ways bricks can be placed on a plot of length (n-1).

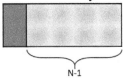

2. If we place the first brick horizontally, the second brick must also be placed horizontally below it as shown in the following figure. The problem is now reduced to finding:
    Number of ways bricks can be placed on a plot of length (n-2).

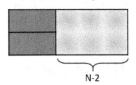

Clearly, this is recursion. The terminating conditions of recursion are:

```
If n==0, there is no way to put a brick.
If n==1, there is only 1 way
    ✓ Place one brick vertically
If n==2, there are 2 possible ways
    ✓ Place both bricks vertically
    ✓ Place both bricks horizontally.
```

Following is the recursive solution for this problem

```
int numOfWays(int n){
  // terminating conditions
  if(n == 0) { return 0; }
  if(n == 1) { return 1; }
  if(n == 2) { return 2; }

  return numOfWays(n-1) + numOfWays(n-2);
}
```

Does this recursion look familiar to you? This is the recursion of Fibonacci numbers. The only difference is in the terminating conditions. This is why we discussed terminating conditions separately from the core recursion.

Because we have similar recursion, converting to DP is super-easy. The dynamic programming solution to this problem will be the same as that of Fibonacci discussed in Code 2.4.

It is a good idea to relate the current problem to a previous one during the interview. You can even talk to the interviewer and inform him about the relationship between the two questions. The ability of a developer to relate and reuse the code is a desirable quality to have that will benefit you during the interview.

Dynamic programming problems can be complex and lengthy, but the good news is that the number of unique DP problems is very few, and most of them can be related to a problem you may have already seen. The first thing in solving a DP is to find the recursive solution to the problem, then think about whether you've seen a similar recursive solution before. If you know a problem with a similar recursion, you can start writing the DP solution using a similar approach and tabulation. *'Similar'* does not mean *'Same'*; please do not ignore any minor differences that may be there in the two recursions.

Finally, I'd like to state that there is no magic formula or shortcut!

The most important aspect is a methodical approach and a lot of practice. As the saying goes, "practise good, practise hard!" In the following section of the book, we will practise a variety of DP problems.

PART-2

BEHOLD THE DP PROBLEMS

The ancient Vedic text of Hinduism has a quotation

एकं सद्विप्रां बहुधा वदन्ति

It implies that different intellectuals visualize and express the same idea in different ways.

In problem-solving also, the same logic may be viewed and comprehended from various perspectives. Each chapter in the second part of this book provides a different perspective to look at Dynamic Programming problems. You may notice that the concepts discussed in the following chapters are not mutually exclusive; this is because a problem and its solution can be looked at from multiple viewpoints. Each chapter discusses one standpoint.

Chapter 4 discusses DP problems related to finding paths. Chapter 5 considers the solution to DP problems based on the number of variables in the problem. In the sixth chapter, we look at each DP problem through the lens of the options available for element in the problem. Chapter 7 contrasts the DP problems with their Greedy alternatives, and the final chapter covers the leftovers.

Path Problems

Chapter 3 discussed a dynamic programming problem related to finding the path. We have already seen a path problem in Example 3.1 that found the total number of unique ways of moving from the top-left cell to the bottom-right cell in a two-dimensional array. The following questions are an extension of Example 3.1. Please review that example before proceeding.

Find path from the End.

Example 4.1: Given a array of order M*N in which we can move in either forward or downward direction (same as Example 3.1). Some of the cells in this matrix are blocked and we cannot pass through them. Determine the total number of ways we can move from the top-left cell (arr[0][0]) to the bottom-right cell. (arr[M-1][N-1]).

In the given diagram (on the right), the cells marked as cross are blocked.

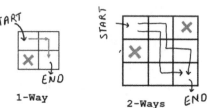

1-Way   2-Ways

This problem's recursion follows the same pattern. We can use the same signature for the function. It accept the destination cell indices and returns the number of ways of reaching that cell from top-left corner cell.

```
int numOfWays(int m, int n)
```

As in Example 3.1, we are either in (m-1,n) or (m,n-1) just before reaching (m,n). If there are x ways to get to (m-1,n) and y ways to get there (m,n-1). Then there are x ways to get to (m,n) from the top and y ways to get to (m,n) from the left. As a result, the total

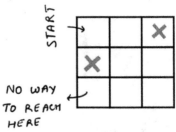

number of ways to reach (m,n) is x+y. An additional check in this question is that if the cell is blocked, there is no way to reach it. It can be taken as an additional terminating condition. We also need to change the logic of finding number of ways of reaching a cell in the first row/col because it may no longer always be 1.

The recursion of Code 3.1 is updated for the given problem in the following code. It assumes a global boolean array having information of whether or not a cell is blocked. The cell (i,j) is blocked if block[i][j] is true.

```
int numOfWays(int m, int n){
  if(m == 0 && n == 0 || block[m][n] == true)
    return 0;
  if(m == 0){          // IN 1st ROW
    return (n==1) ? 1 : numOfWays(m, n-1);
  }
  if(n == 0){          // IN 1st COL
    return (m==1) ? 1 : numOfWays(m-1, n);
  }

  return numOfWays(m-1, n) + numOfWays(m, n-1);
}
```

Code 4.1

The time taken by this recursion of Code 4.1 is $O(2^n)$ and the function call tree in the worst case is same as the function call tree of Code 3.1. The memorization of Code 4.1 is also similar to the memoization in Code 3.2 using a similar two-dimensional array as cache.

Code 4.2 has the dynamic programming solution of this problem. This DP solution takes $O(m.n)$ time and populate the matrix in the opposite direction. It is a significant improvement over exponential-time recursive solution of Code 4.1.

```
int numOfWays(int m, int n){
   int arr[m+1][n+1];

   arr[0][0] = 0;
   for(int i=1; i<=m; i++){
      if(block[i][0] == true)
         arr[i][0] = 0;
      else
         arr[i][0] = (i==1)?1:arr[i-1][0];
   }
   for(int i=1; i<=n; i++){
      if(block[0][i] == true)
         arr[0][i] = 0;
      else
         arr[0][i] = (i==1)?1:arr[0][i-1];
   }

   for(int i=1; i<=m; i++){
      for(int j=1; j<=n; j++)
         if(block[i][j] == 1)
            arr[i][j] = 0;
         else
            arr[i][j] = arr[i-1][j] + arr[i][j-1];
   }
   return arr[m][n];
}
```

Terminating Condition of recursion becomes initialization in DP

Logic remains the same

Code 4.2

Example 4.2: Given a two-dimensional array cost[][] of order M*N where cost[i][j] represents the cost of passing through the cell (i,j). The total cost to reach a particular cell is the sum of the costs of all the cells in the path (including the first and last cells in the path). You can only move either downward or rightward. Given that a cost is always positive, find the minimum cost of moving from the top-left cell to the bottom-right cell of the given matrix.

For example, Figure 4.1 shows the cost array and the minimum cost path of going from (0,0) to (2,3). The cost of the minimum cost path is 12 (the sum of costs of all the cells in the path):

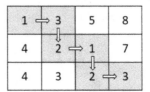

| Cost Matrix | | | | | MinCostPath |

Figure 4.1

This problem is also related to the previous one. In recursion, the larger problem is defined in terms of smaller subproblems of the same type.

- **Larger Problem:** Find minimum path cost till cell (2,3)
- **Smaller Problems-1:** Find minimum path cost till cell (2,2)
- **Smaller Problems-2:** Find minimum path cost till cell (1,3)

Structurally, smaller problems are exactly same as the larger problem with different parameters. The same function, that solves the large problem can also be used to the smaller problems. Hence, Recursion!

First, find the solutions to smaller problems, i.e the minimum cost to reach cell (2,2) and (1,3), let it be x and y respectively. Now, cell (2,3) can only be reached via (2,2) or (1,3). The minimum cost of reaching cell (2,3) will be

MINIMUM(x, Y) + Cost[2][3]

Following are the code statements of above logic

```
int minPathCost(int cost[M][N], int m, int n){
    ... ...
    int x = minPathCost(cost, m-1, n);
    int y = minPathCost(cost, m, n-1);
    return (getMin(x,y) + cost[m][n]);
}
```

The function getMin returns minimum of two integers. Let us add the following terminating conditions in the above code:

1. If m=0 and n=0, it means our destination is top-left cell itself. There is only one cell, return the cost of cell (0,0).

2. If m=0 and n≠0, we are in the top Row but not at (0,0). There is only one way to reach this cell and that is from the left because there is no way to reach this cell from the top. Calculate the minPathCost of cell on the left and add the cost of current cell to it.

3. If m≠0 and n=0, we are in the first column but not at (0,0). There is only one way to reach this cell and that is from the top because there is no way to reach this cell from the left. Calculate the minPathCost of cell above it and add the cost of current cell to it.

Following is the complete code.

```
int minPathCost(int[][] cost, int m, int n){
    if(m == 0 && n == 0)   // At cell (0,0)
        return cost[0][0];

    if(m == 0) // FIRST ROW
        return minPathCost(cost,m,n-1) + cost[0][n];

    if(n == 0) // FIRST COLUMN
        return minPathCost(cost,m-1,n) + cost[m][0];

    int x = minPathCost(cost, m-1, n);
    int y = minPathCost(cost, m, n-1);
    return (getMin(x,y) + cost[m][n]);
}
```

Code: 4.3

Observe the Optimal substructure property in the preceding code. The optimal solution of larger problem depends on the optimal solutions of smaller subproblems. Code 4.3 has overlapping subproblems as well.

The following diagram shows function call tree for M=2, N=3. The numbers in each node represent the values of parameters M and N for the function call of that node. The diagram is not complete for the sake of saving space, but in this diagram itself, we are computing the minPathCost of reaching cell (1,2) twice. All the function calls in the subtree with cell (1, 2) are duplicate. Height of this tree is $O(m+n)$ and number of nodes in the tree are exponential, $O(2^n)$. Time taken by Code 4.3 too is $O(2^n)$.

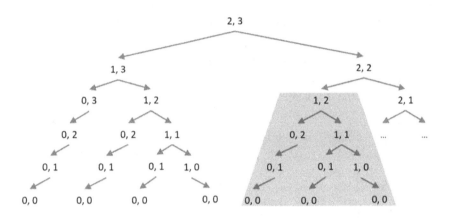

Memoized Approach (Recursion + Remember)

The solution of `minPathCost` for cell `(i,j)` can be stored in a two-dimensional array at index `(i,j)`. When `minPathCost` of cell `(i,j)` is needed again, do a look-up into the array. The array `c` in the following code is used as a cache memory to memorize the above recursion:

```
int minCost(int[][] c, int[][] cost, int m, int n){
   // If value for cell (m,n) is already computed.
   if(c[m][n] != 0)
      return c[m][n];

   if(m == 0 && n == 0)
      c[m][n] = cost[0][0];
   else if(m == 0)
      c[m][n] = minCost(cost,m,n-1)+cost[0][n];
   else if(n == 0)
      c[m][n] = minCost(cost,m-1,n)+cost[m][0];
   else{
      int x = minCost(cost, m-1, n);
      int y = minCost(cost, m, n-1);
      c[m][n] = getMin(x,y) + cost[m][n]);
   }
   return c[m][n];
}
```

Code: 4.4

When `minCost` is computed for any cell `(i,j)` for the first time, store the value in cache at `c[i][j]`. Before computing the `minCost` for any cell, check if that value already exists in the cache or not. If already computed, just return that value without recomputing it again.

Code 4.4 does not have overlapping subproblems and takes $O(n^2)$ time. For a larger matrix, this difference between recursion and memorization is substantial.

Bottom-Up Dynamic Solution

The data structure used in the DP solution will be a two-dimensional array because there are two variables (also that is what we used as cache in memoization in Code 4.4). Use the terminating conditions of recursion in Code 4 to initialize the first row and first column of this array. `minCost` of $(0,0)$ is same as `cost[0][0]`

1			

The direction of application of logic in DP is opposite to that of recursion. i.e in DP we will populate this array bottom-up starting from $(0,0)$ to (m,n) [9] and keep finding `minCost` for all the cells in the way. First let's populate the first row and first column of the array.

First Row: A cell in the first row can only be reached by moving forward from $(0,0)$. Minimum cost to reach a cell in the first row is the sum of costs of all cells till that cell (including current cell).

1	4	9	17

First Col: Similarly, minimum cost to reach a cell in the first column is the sum of costs of all the cells in that column till the current cell.

1	4	9	17
5			
9			

---

[9] Do not get confused by the name 'Bottom-Up'. It means that we are moving from the base case (or source) to the advanced case (or destination).

After populating the first row and the first column, populate the rest of the array. Calculate the minCost of a specific cell by adding minCost of the cell above it and minCost of the cell on the left of it starting from the top-left. The logic employed is the same as that used in recursion and memoization.

```
a[i][j] = getMin(a[i-1][j], a[i][j-1]) + cost[i][j]
```

Following is the complete code of Dynamic Programming.

```
int minCost(int[][] cost, int M, int N){
    int[][] a = new int[M][N];
    a[0][0] = cost[0][0];

    for(int j=1; j<N ; j++) // FIRST ROW
        a[0][j] = a[0][j-1] + cost[0][j];

    for(int i=1; i<M ; i++) // FIRST COLUMN
        a[i][0] = a[i-1][0] + cost[i][0];

    // Filling other cells
    for(int i=1; i<M; i++)
        for(int j=1; j<N; j++)
            a[i][j] = getMin(a[i-1][j], a[i][j-1]) +
                    cost[i][j];

    return a[M-1][N-1];
}
```

Code 4.5

Code 4.5 does not use recursion and runs in $O(n^2)$ time. It is a huge improvement over the previous two versions, Recursion and Memoization.

Each cell of final array, a store the minimum cost to reach that cell from $(0, 0)$. The final values in the array are as follows,

1	4	9	17
5	6	7	14
9	9	9	12

The minimum cost to reach the last cell is 12.

Find the Path

What if the question is not to just find the minimum cost but to also print the cheapest path?

After populating the minCost path array using Code 4.5, we know that the minimum cost is 12. The path of minimum cost is also hidden in the array itself. Start with the last cell, (2, 3) and backtrack using the same logic trace back the path till (0,0). The following function receives the array populated by Code 4.5 and print the minimum cost path till the bottom-right cell of the array in reverse order.

```
public static void printMinCostPath(int[][] mc){
    int m = mc.length-1;
    int n = mc[0].length-1;
    while(true){
        System.out.print("("+m+","+n+") ");

        if(m == 0 && n == 0) // REACHED THE TOP-LEFT
            break;
        if(m == 0)                 // IN FIRST ROW
            n--;
        else if( n == 0)           // IN FIRST COL
            m--;
        else{
            if(a[m-1][n] < a[m][n-1])
                m--;
            else
                n--;
        }
    }
}
```

The output of the above code is
```
(2,3) (2,2) (1,2) (1,1) (0,1) (0,0)
```

Use a Stack to print the path in forward order. Or just push the cells in a vector and print it in reverse order.

Question 4.1: What will be the logic if you are allowed to move in three directions, right, down, and diagonally as shown in the following figure.

Question 4.2: Modify Example 3.1, so that it prints all unique paths (instead of just counting them). For example, in a 2*2 array, there are two ways of going from top-left cell to bottom-right cell as shown below:

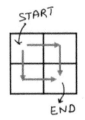

Path-1: (0,0) ⟶ (0,1) ⟶ (1,1)

Path-2: (0,0) ⟶ (1,0) ⟶ (1,1)

Question 4.3: The road network of a city is in the form of a grid. There are roads after every kilometre along the x-axis and y-axis, and every intersection has a roundabout, where you can take any turn you like, as shown in the following figure:

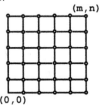

Answer the following question.

  i. In how many unique ways can you go from (0, 0) to (m, n).

 ii. Some of the roads are blocked because of some ongoing construction work (cross in the following diagram shows roadblock). In how many unique ways can a person now go from (0, 0) to (m, n)?

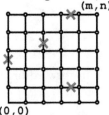

iii. Given the traffic on all the roads between two roundabouts (in terms of average time taken) and a point (m,n); Find the fastest route from (0, 0) to (m, n). In the following diagram, if you want to go from (0, 0) to (1, 1), going via (0,1) is faster and will take 8 time (5+3) in comparison to going via (1,0). Going upward may appear to be faster at (0,0), but doing so will trap you in a much bigger traffic between (1,0) to (1,1).

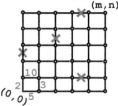

Do these questions remind you of the previous example in this chapter? Congratulations, you have completed a very basic Google Maps POC. You could argue that all these problems involve straight roads. Our road network is not a square grid. However, it is intended to be a proof of concept in which reasonable assumptions can be made. The next example solves a more generic path problem.

Example 4.3: Given the diagram of roads connecting multiple points in a city, and the travel time between any two points. Determine the shortest route (and time) from **A** to **J**.

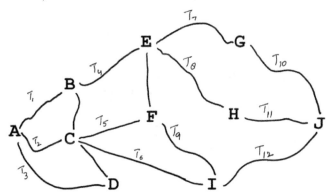

This is a generic path problem with a road network that is like real-world roads. Let us start with the recursion. If we consider the source **A** to be always fixed, the original problem is:

Find the min time to reach J

Just before reaching **J**, a person is at either one of the three points, **G**, **H** or

I. We can use recursion to solve the following three sub-problems:

    ✓   `minTime1` = *Find the min time to reach* **G**
    ✓   `minTime2` = *Find the min time to reach* **H**
    ✓   `minTime3` = *Find the min time to reach* **I**

The solution to original problem is the minimum of the following 3 values:

`minTime1+`T_{10} , `minTime2+`T_{11} , `minTime3+`T_{12}

This is recursion. The only problem with the above recursion is that it can lead to infinite recursion. However, this can be easily fixed using a visited HashSet. You may also think of memorizing this recursion or converting it to bottom-up DP to improve the performance. Here, you may prefer to use a HashMap as cache instead of an array. The key of HashMap is the point in the map and value is the minimum cost to reach that point from **A**. This minimum cost may be computed incrementally the way we compute the shortest path in a graph using Bellman Ford Algorithm.

Example 4.4: Find the total number of unique ways to climb the nth step from the floor (Step-0) if you can climb either 1 or 2 steps at a time. Following figure shows the results for n=1, n=2 and n=3.

If n=4, there are 5 different ways in which you can go to step-4.

Like previous examples, focus on the end point, i.e Step-n. Just reaching Step-n, a person is either at Step-$(n-1)$ and climbed 1 step to reach Step-n, or at Step-$(n-2)$ and climbed 2 steps at to reach Step-n. If a person can reach Step-(n-1) in x distinct ways and Step-$(n-2)$ in y distinct ways, then he can reach step-n in $(x+y)$ unique ways.

    `numOfWays(n) = numOfWays(n-1) + numOfWays(n-2)` .

This sounds like the recursion of Fibonacci discussed in Code 2.1. The only difference is in the terminating conditions. Following is the recursive code,

```
int numOfWays(int n){
    // terminating conditions
    if(n == 0) { return 0; }
    if(n == 1) { return 1; }
    if(n == 2) { return 2; }

    return numOfWays(n-1) + numOfWays(n-2);
}
```

The DP solution will be exactly same as that of Fibonacci, except for the initializations.

Example 4.5: Consider a game where a player can score 3, 5 or 10 points in one move. Given a total score N, find the number of unique ways to reach this score (of N). For example, if N = 13, output should 5 because there are following 5 ways to reach to the score of 13

(3, 10), (3, 5, 5), (5, 3, 5), (5, 5, 3), (10, 3)

This may not appear to be a straightforward path-problem. However, there is a striking resemblance, and the question can easily be rephrased to find distinct paths to the nth step when you can take 3, 5, or 10 steps at a times.

The top-down (recursive) solution to this problem is,

```
#of ways to score N = #of ways to score (N-10) +
                      #of ways to score (N-5)  +
                      #of ways to score (N-3)
```

With the following two terminating conditions:
```
    1. #of ways to score negative == 0
    2. #of ways to score 0 == 1
```

Following is the code for above recursion,
```
int waysToScore(int n){
    if(n<0) { return 0; }
    if(n == 0) { return 1; }

    return waysToScore(n-10) +
           waysToScore(n-5) +
           waysToScore(n-3);
```

}

The code above solves subproblems multiple times. The function-call tree for n=13, is shown in the following figure. It is not complete, but it illustrates the overlaps. As n becomes larger, the number of overlaps grows exponentially. In the worst case, this code takes exponential time, $O(n^3)$.

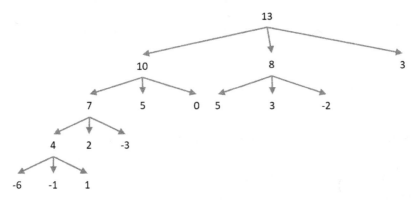

Code 4.6 converts this recursion to bottom-up dynamic programming solution. It uses one-dimensional array, arr and store number of ways to score k at index k in the array.

```
int waysToScore(int n){
    // arr[i] will store numberOfWays to score i.
    int arr[n+1], i;

    for(i=0; i<n+1; i++)
        arr[i] = 0;

    arr[0] = 1;

    for(i=1; i<=n; i++)
    {
        if(i-3 >= 0)
            arr[i] += arr[i-3];
        if(i-5 >= 0)
            arr[i] += arr[i-5];
        if(i-10 >= 0)
            arr[i] += arr[i-10];
    }
    return arr[n];
}
```

Code 4.6

In most of the path problems, we follow the same approach.

1. To find all possible ways of reaching a point (or moving away from a point), find the points where the person can possibly be just before reaching the end point (of just after the starting point).
2. For each of these points, solve the problem recursively, and
3. Add the required terminating conditions.

Question 4.4: In Example 4.5, in how many ways can we get to a particular score if `(10, 3)` and `(3, 10)` are considered same?

Question 4.5: Minimum Chess Moves problem. In the game of chess, a Knight can move 2.5 steps (a square that can be reached by moving two squares horizontally and one square vertically, or two squares vertically and one square horizontally). Figure 4.2 (A) shows all possible moves of a knight. The King can only move one step (either horizontally, vertically or diagonally). Valid moves of a king are shown in Figure 4.2 (B).

We created a unique piece (**P**) that can move like a knight or like a king. All valid moves of this new piece **P** are shown in Figure 4.2(C). It is union of moves of Knight and King.

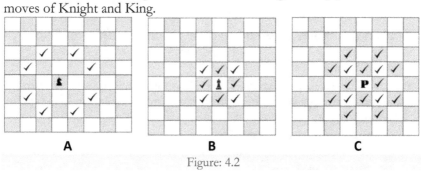

Figure: 4.2

The piece **P** is present in a cell (source), and we want to move it to another cell (destination). What is the minimum number of **P** can make to go from source to destination.

Example 4.6 (Hamiltonian Path): A Hamiltonian Path in a Graph is a path that visits each vertex exactly once. The problem of determining whether a graph contains a Hamiltonian Path, as well as the problem of finding all Hamiltonian Paths in a graph, is NP-complete. Given a Graph, Find whether or not a Hamiltonian Path exists in the Graph.

Graph given in Figure 4.3 (A) has three Hamiltonian Paths, two of which are highlighted in B) and C). But the Graph of Figure 4.3 (D) does not have a Hamiltonian path.

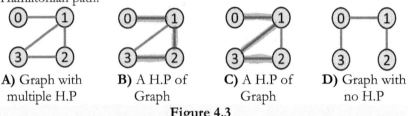

A) Graph with multiple H.P   **B)** A H.P of Graph   **C)** A H.P of Graph   **D)** Graph with no H.P

Figure 4.3

The Hamiltonian path problem is NP-hard, which means that it is computationally difficult to find an optimal solution for large graphs. However, there are several algorithms and heuristics that can be used to find a Hamiltonian path in specific types of graphs or under certain conditions. Some of the most common approaches include:

✓ **Backtracking**: This involves starting from a vertex and exploring all possible paths until a Hamiltonian path is found or all paths have been exhausted.

✓ **Branch and bound**: This method involves searching for a Hamiltonian path by bounding the search space and exploring only those paths that are likely to lead to a solution.

✓ **Approximation algorithms**: These algorithms can be used to find a suboptimal solution to the Hamiltonian path problem in a faster time than exact algorithms.

✓ **Local search heuristics**: These algorithms involve starting from an initial solution and making small changes to the solution in an attempt to improve it.

✓ **Dynamic programming**: This involves breaking down the problem into smaller subproblems and using their solutions to find the solution to the larger problem.

In general, the choice of algorithm will depend on the specific characteristics of the graph being analyzed, such as the number of vertices and edges, the degree of each vertex, and the structure of the graph.

A Hamiltonian Path is also a permutation of the vertices of the given graph such that there is an edge between any two adjacent vertices in the permutation. A straightforward solution is to find all possible permutations and for each permutation check that presence of edge between the adjacent vertices. Total number of possible permutations of N vertices are N! and it will take O(N) time to check each permutation. In the worst case this logic will take O(N*N!) time.

Bellman, Held, and Karp proposed a dynamic programming algorithm for determining whether or not a Hamiltonian Path exists in a graph.

For every subset, **S** of vertices check whether there exist a path that visits all (and ONLY) the vertices in **S** exactly once. For all such paths, do this for every vertex, **v** in **S** such that the path ends in **v**. If **v** has a neighbour **w** in **S**, and there is a path that visits each vertex in **S-{v}** exactly once and ends in **w**. If such a path exists, adding the edge **w-v** to it will extend the path to visit **v**, and the new path will also visit every vertex in **S**.

Consider the Graph in Figure 4.3(A). Let
S = {0,1,2} and v = 2

A path exists in {0,1,2} that visits each node exactly once and ends in **2**. Also 2 has a neighbour **1** in **S**, such that there is a path that visits each vertex in the set **S-{2}={0,1}** exactly once and ends at **1**.

We have not yet discussed the logic fully, but you can see the Recursion and the overlapping subproblems and hence the scope for Memoization in the above approach. Let us directly jump to the DP solution

Dynamic Programming Solution

Define a two-dimensional table dp[][] of size (n x 2^n), where n is the number of vertices in the graph and 2^n is the possible number of subsets. For each vertex there are two option:

-   Include the vertex in the subset
-   Do not include the vertex in the subset

Bitmasking can used to represent a subset. For example, the binary representation of 9 is 1001, that represent the subset {0,3}. Only include the bits corresponding to 1 in the binary representation of the number. That ways we will have the mast from 0000 to 1111 for four vertices.This gives us the total number of subsets as 2^n.

dp[j][i] store the information if there is a path that ends at j and visits each vertex in subset represented by mask i.

If there is only one vertex in the subset, then there is a path that visits every vertex in that subset and ends at that vertex because there is only one vertex. For each i (0<=i<N)

```
dp[i][2ⁱ] = true
```

Every cell of dp is initialized to False.

```
for(int i=0; i < Math.pow(2,n); i++)
   for(int j=0; j < n; j++)
     dp[j][i] = false;
for(int i=0; i < n; i++)
   dp[i][ Math.pow(2,i)] = true;
```

`Math.pow` is a library function used to find exponent.

mask Vertex	0000	0001	0010	0011	0100	0101	0110	0111	1000	1001	1010	1011	1100	1101	1110	1111
	0	1	2	3	4	5	6	7	8	9	10	11	12	13	14	15
0	0	1	0	0	0	0	0	0	0	0	0	0	0	0	0	0
1	0	0	1	0	0	0	0	0	0	0	0	0	0	0	0	0
2	0	0	0	0	1	0	0	0	0	0	0	0	0	0	0	0
3	0	0	0	0	0	0	0	0	1	0	0	0	0	0	0	0

The next step is for each vertex j present in every subset, check which of the vertices from 0 to N-1 in that subset is the neighbour of j. For each such neighbour vertex k, check the value of cell dp[k][i.XOR.2ʲ], where i is the subset. The bits in the binary value of i.XOR.2ʲ is same as that of i except for the jᵗʰ bit. So i.XOR.2ʲ actually represent the subset S-{j} and cell dp[k][i.XOR.2ʲ] represents if there is a path that visits each vertex in the subset S-{j} exactly once and ends in k. If such a path is there then adding edge k-j extends that path to visit each vertex in S exactly once and end in j. If such a path exists then set dp[j][i] to true.

```
for(int i=0; i < Math.pow(2,n); i++) // SUBSET - i
   for(int j=0; j < n; j++)               // Vertex - j
     if(getBit(i, j) == 1)     // j'TH BIT IN i IS SET
       for(int k=0; k < n; k++)
         if(j!=k && getBit(i,k)==1 && adj[k][j]==true)
           if(dp[k][i^Math.pow(2,j)] == true)
             dp[j][i] = true;
             break;
```

Using the above logic the Matrix will be populated as follows. Number of Hamiltonian paths in the given graph is equal to the number of cells in the last column with a true value (in this case 1). The last column represent the orignal set S that has all the vertices (because all bits in the binary representation of 2^n-1 are 1. A cell in the last column means whether of not a hamiltonian path exist that ends in the vertex represented by that row.

mask → Vertex ↓	0000 0	0001 1	0010 2	0011 3	0100 4	0101 5	0110 6	0111 7	1000 8	1001 9	1010 10	1011 11	1100 12	1101 13	1110 14	1111 15
0	0	1	0	1	0	0	0	0	0	0	0	1	0	0	0	1
1	0	0	1	1	0	0	1	0	0	0	1	0	0	0	1	0
2	0	0	0	0	1	0	1	0	0	0	0	0	1	0	1	1
3	0	0	0	0	0	0	0	0	1	0	1	1	1	0	1	1

According to the above matrix, there is are three Hamiltonian paths each ending at vertex 0, 2, and 3 respectively.

Question 4.6: The previous Example 4.6 does not find the Hamiltonian path; it just checks whether such path exist or not. How can you modify the logic to print a path? Extend it further to print all possible paths.

Question 4.7: A Hamiltonian Cycle is formed when there is an edge from the last vertex to the first vertex in a Hamiltonian path. Determine whether or not a Hamiltonian cycle exists in the given graph.

Find path from the beginning.

In some questions, the recursion finds the path from the beginning rather than the end. Consider the following example,

Example 4.7 (Minimum jumps to reach the end): Given an array in which each element represents the maximum number of steps one can jump forward from that index. You are initially at index 0, find the minimum number of jumps required to reach the last index of the array starting . If you cannot reach the last index, return -1. For example, If the input array is

```
Int[] arr = {2, 3, 1, 1, 4}
```

In 2 jumps, one can go from the first index to the last.

The first jump is only one step (even though you can also jump 2 steps because `arr[0]=2`). After the first jump, you will be at `arr[1]`. Now jump 3 steps to the last index.

Recursion

The recursion is very straightforward if we start from the beginning of the array.
```
minJumps(i) = getMin( minJumps(i+k), 1<=k<=arr[i])
```

Following is the recursive function
```
int minJumps(int arr[], int i){
  if(i == arr.length-1)
    return 0;

  if(arr[i] == 0)      // IMPOSSIBLE TO MOVE FORWARD
    return -1;

  int minVal = Integer.MAX_VALUE;
  for (int k=i+1; k<arr.length && k<=i+arr[i]; k++) {
    int val = minJumps(arr, k);
    if(val != -1 && val+1 < minVal)
      minVal = val + 1;
  }

  if(minVal == Integer.MAX_VALUE)
    return -1;
  else
    return minVal;
}
```

This code takes exponential time and has overlapping subproblems and optimal substructure. The overlapping subproblems can be removed using memoization. A one dimensional array can be used as a cache and once we find the minimum number of jumps from index i to the end of the array, store it in `cache[i]` and then reuse it when needed.

Dynamic Programming Solution

The DP solution should use a one dimensional array (because that is what we will use as a cache in memoization) and use the logic of recursion in opposite direction to populate the array. `dp[i]` will store the minimum number of jumps required to reach index i.

Note the difference between top-down and bottom-up again. In Top down memoization, we stored the number of ways to go from the i'th index to the final destination whereas in the bottom-up DP the i'th index stores the minimum number of jumps required to reach index-i from the beginning of the array.

```
int minJumps(int[] arr)
{
  int n = arr.length;
  int[] dp = new int[n];
  for(int i=0; i<n; i++)
    dp[i] = Integer.MAX_VALUE;

  dp[0] = 0;

  for(int i=0; i<n-1; i++) {
    for(int j=i+1; j<n && j<=arr[i]+i; j++) {
      if(dp[j] > dp[i]+1){
        dp[j] = dp[i]+1;
      }
    }
  }
  return (dp[n-1] == Integer.MAX_VALUE)? -1: dp[n-1];
}
```

The minimum number of steps to reach a point is initialized to positive infinity. If we find a smaller value using the logic of recursion, update it else keep it as it is.

5

Number of variables

Some Dynamic Programming solutions make decisions based on the number of variables in the problem. This chapter focuses on those decisions by examining specific Dynamic programming problems. After reading this chapter, please relook at the questions discussed in the previous chapters from the point of view of the number of variables in that problem.

We saw in the previous chapter how array used in a DP solution depends on the number of variables. A one-dimensional array is (generally) used in DP solutions of single-variable problems, while a two-dimensional array is used in most of the two-variable DP problems.

One-variable Problems

This section focuses on single-variable DP problems. After that, we will look at the DP problems with two variables. Because all the examples in this section have a single variable, the dynamic programming solution uses a one-dimensional array.

The Fibonacci series problem in Chapter 2 was a one-variable problem. Similarly, Code 3.7 of the minimum cost path problem approached the problem as a one-variable problem and solved it with a one-dimensional array. In contrast, Code 3.5 used a two-dimensional array for the same problem because it perceived it as a two-variable problem. Let us look at few more single-variable problems.

Example 5.1 (Cutting the Rod): Given a rod of a certain length and an array of prices for selling a rod of specific lengths in the market. Find a way to cut the rod into multiple pieces such that it maximizes the value we can get by selling those pieces in the market. For example, if the market price of different lengths of rods are as follows:

Length	1	2	3	4	5	6	7	8
Price	1	5	8	9	10	17	17	20

If we have a rod of length 4, we can sell it in the market as is (without cutting it into pieces) for a value of 9. However, if we cut the road into two pieces of length of 2 each, each piece can be sold separately for 5 each, for a total value of 10. As a result, it is preferable to sell the rod after cutting it into two pieces rather than as a single piece.

However, we are unsure whether cutting the rod into two equal pieces is the best solution. Following table lists all possible ways to cut a rod of length 4 along with the total market value of each option.

Length of each part	Total Value
4	9
1, 3	1 + 8 = 9
2, 2	5 + 5 = 10
1, 1, 2	1 + 1 + 5 = 7
1, 1, 1, 1	1 + 1 + 1 + 1 = 4

The table does not show duplicate rows. For example, if the lengths of the first and second pieces are 1 and 3, it will give the same value as if the first piece is 3 and the second piece is 1. It is not permutation, but combination.

From the above table, it is clear that cutting the rod of length 4 in two equal pieces of length 2 each gives us the maximum value (assuming, cutting the rod does not incur any cost and does not result in any wastage). Every other way will give us less value. There may be more than one ways to get the maximum value. Now, let us form the solution step-by-step.

Recursion

The recursive solution to this problem examines all possible combinations along with the value associated with each combination and return the maximum of all these values. At the most basic level, there are two options for any iron rod:

    i.   Do not cut the rod at all

    ii.   Cut the rod into at least two pieces

There are several sub-options in the second option. If we want to cut the rod into at least two pieces, the first piece can be 1 or 2 or 3 or 4... or n-1 in length. Fix the length of first piece with each of these options one at a time, and then try to get the maximum value out of the second piece.

```
// value[k] = value of rod of length k
int cutRod(int[] value, int n){
  if(n <= 0)
     return 0;

  int maxValue = value[n]; // NOT CUTTING THE ROD
  for (int i=1; i<n; i++){ // 1st PIECE IS OF LENGTH i
    int tempVal = value[i] + cutRod(value, n-i);

    if(tempVal > maxValue)
       maxValue = tempVal;
  }
  return maxValue;
}
```

Code: 5.1

Following diagram shows the function call tree of Code 5.1 for n=4 .

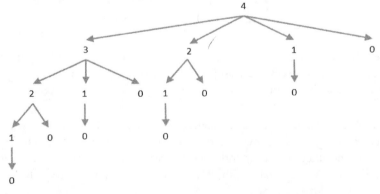

Code 5.1 will provide the most optimal solution, but as shown in the diagram, we are computing the maxValue for one size multiple times (overlapping subproblems). The maxValue for length 2 is computed twice. If N is large there will be many overlapping subproblems. The solution in Code 5.1 takes exponential time because of these overlapping subproblems.

Memoization

Memorization store the result of smaller subproblems in a cache when a subproblem is solved for the first time and then reuse this result when the same subproblem needs to be solved again.

Code 5.2 stores the results of subproblems in a one-dimensional array maxValues of size n+1. For the sake of simplicity, let us assume that this array is defined globally. The **i**'th index of this array holds the maximum value for a rod of length **i**. If maximum value for a rod of length **i** is already computed, then it is looked up in this array, else it is computed and stored at maxValues[i].

```
// holds max value for rod of length i at index i.
int[] maxValues = new int[N];

int cutRod(int[] value, int n){
  if (n <= 0)
    return 0;

  // If maxValue is not already computed
  if(maxValues[n] == 0){
    return maxValues[n];

    maxValues[n] = value[n];

    for (int i=1; i<n; i++){
      int tempVal = value[i] + cutRod(value, n-i);
      if(tempVal > maxValue)
        maxValue = tempVal;
    }
  }
  return maxValues[n];
}
```

Code: 5.2

The above code runs in polynomial time, $O(n^2)$, but it is not the most optimal code. A better solution would be to use DP and solve the problem bottom-up without using recursion as shown next.

Dynamic Programming Solution

In the dynamic programming, we solve the problem bottom-up, beginning with a rod of length 0, and moving forward to a rod of length n. The same logic from recursion is used to populate the array maxValues in forward direction starting from the beginning.

The initial index of the array is initialized using the terminating condition of recursion.

```
int cutRod(int[] value, int n){
   int[] maxValues = new int[n+1]; // FROM MEMOIZATION
   maxValues[0] = 0; // TERMINATING COND. OF RECURSION

   // CALCULATE MAX VALUE FOR LENGTH i
   for(int i = 1; i<=n; i++){
     maxValues[i] = value[i];
     for (int j=1; j<i; j++){
       int tempVal = value[j] + maxValues[i-j];
       if(tempVal > maxValues[i])
         maxValues[i] = tempVal;
     }
   }

   return maxValues[n];
}
```

Code: 5.3

Code 5.3 populated following values in the array left to right for n=8:
maxValues = {0, 1, 5, 8, 10, 13, 17, 18, 22}

These values are populated for the following prices of the lengths

Length	1	2	3	4	5	6	7	8
Price	1	5	8	9	10	17	17	20

This DP solution takes $O(n^2)$ time, which is significantly faster than the exponential time recursive solution. Note that the logic of this solution is very similar to the logic of train-stations problem discussed in Example 3.2. There were two solutions, one using one-variable problem (only the destination station was variable and source was fixed at Station-0) and the other solution was using two-variables (both source station and destination stations are variables).

In this example, only one variable make sense. So it can relate to only one variation of the solution and not both of them. This is one of the reasons why we should look at every possible solution of a problem.

Two-Variable Problems

The previous problem was a single variable problem like the Fibonacci sequence and its variations. The path problems in Examples 3.1 and 4.1 had two variables. Their DP solution used a two-dimensional array with possible values for the first variable along one dimension and possible values for the second variable along the other. The following examples look at problems with two variables.

Example 5.2 (Minimum Edit Distance): The words **computer** and **commuter** are very similar, and if a single character **p** is **replaced** with **m,** the two strings will become same. Similarly, word **sport** can become **sort** by **deleting** one character, **p**, or equivalently, **sort** can become **sport** with the **insertion** of **p**.

The Minimum Edit Distance between two strings is defined as the minimum number of operations required to convert one string to another. The operations are restricted to one of the three options, Insert, Delete, or Update. Given two strings s1 and s2 and the following three operations on s1. If APIs of three operations are,

   i. `Insert(char ch, int pos)` : Insert character ch at position pos
  ii. `Delete(int pos)` : Removes a character at position pos
 iii. `Update(int pos, char ch` : Replace character at pos with ch

and all the above operations are of equal cost, find the minimum number of operations required to convert s1 to s2.

For Example: if the two strings are CAT and CAR then the minimum edit distance is 1. Update character at position 2 with 'R'.

$$
\begin{array}{ccc}
C & A & T \\
 & & \downarrow \\
C & A & R \\
 & & \text{CHANGE}
\end{array}
$$

We may also convert CAT to CAR using the following two operations, performed in this order

```
s1.Insert('R', 3);    // s1 becomes CATR
s1.Delete(2);         // s1 becomes CAR = s2
```

Similarly, if the two input strings are, SUNDAY and SATURDAY, then minimum edit distance is 3.

Recursive Solution

In most recursion that involve two arrays, two strings, two linked list, or any two collections, we focus on only one (current) element from each collection in a function, leave the rest to recursion. In the given problem, we have two strings, so each recursive function call should focus on one character from each string. Let us take the following signature of the function.

```
int minEditDist(char[] s1, char[] s2, int i, int j)
```

Parameters i and j represent the current indices of the two strings, s1 and s2, Start with comparing the first character of s1 with first character of s2, i.e i=0 and j=0, there are following possibilities,

- **s1[i] == s2[j]**
  If the current characters are the same, do nothing for this position and compute the minimum edit distance between the remaining parts of two strings (ignoring the current character of each), i.e
  ```
  miEditDist(s1, s2, i+1, j+1)
  ```

- **s1[i] != s2[j]**
  If they are not same, perform all three operations on the current character of s1:

  - **Delete s1[i]** and find the minimum edit distance between s2 and rest of s1 (starting from index, i+1). i.e Find the minimum edit distance between the two strings s1 and s2 starting from i+1 and j respectively.
    ```
    miEditDist(s1, s2, i+1, j)
    ```

  - **Update s1[i]** to be same as the current character of s2, (s2[j]) and then find the minimum edit distance between rest of the two strings ignoring current characters of each string (because they are same now).
    ```
    miEditDist(s1, s2, i+1, j+1)
    ```

- **Insert s2[j]**, the current character of s2 at the current index in s1. After insertion, the current characters of s1 and s2 are same and hence can be ignored. Note that we are not actually inserting (because that takes O(n) time) but assuming that the character is inserted. Now find the minimum edit distance between rest of the two strings,

  miEditDist(s1, s2, i, j+1)

In all the three cases, we reduce the length of either one or both the strings by one and then find the minimum edit distance between the remaining two strings. All three recursion will give us the minimum edit distance when that operation is performed on the string. Pick the minimum out of these three results and add one to it to get the answer. One is added because no matter which of the three operations (Delete, Update or Insert) gives the minimum value, one operation is definitely performed.

Following is the code for above recursion,

```
int minEditDist(char[] s1, char[] s2, int i, int j){
  // If s1 finished, insert rest of s2 at the end
  if(i == s1.length)
    return s2.length-j; // REMAINING CHAR IN s2

  // If s2 finished, delete remaining char from s1
  if(j == s2.length)
    return s1.length-i; // REMAINING CHAR IN s1

  // IF CURRENT CHAR IN BOTH ARE SAME
  if(s1[i] == s2[j])
    return minEditDist(s1, s2, i+1, j+1);

  // IF CURRENT CHAR ARE NOT SAME. TRY ALL 3 OPTIONS
  int a, b, c;
  a = minEditDist(s1, s2, i+1, j);     // DELETE
  b = minEditDist(s1, s2, i+1, j+1);   // UPDATE
  c = minEditDist(s1, s2, i, j+1);     // INSERT

  // RETURN THE MIN OF 3 VALUES PLUS 1
  return getMinimum(a, b, c) + 1;
```

}

Code: 5.4

Assuming there is a `getMinimum` function to find the minimum of three integer values. Code 5.4 takes exponential time, i.e $O(n^3)$ in the worst case, and has many overlapping sub-problems as shown in the following function call tree. The two values at each node of the tree represent string lengths rather than index values.

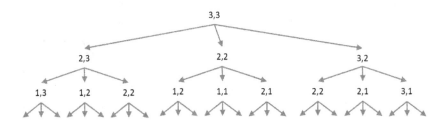

The diagram represents function calls for two string of length 3 each for the worst-case scenario when no two characters matches, e.x. `"ABC"` & `"XYZ"`. The best case takes $O(n)$ time when both the strings are same.

Memoization

There are overlapping subproblems as shown in the function call tree. For two strings of lengths m and n respectively, we want to store the minimum edit distance value corresponding to each `(i,j)` where `0<=i<=m` and `0<=j<=n`. A natural choice for cache to store the solution to subproblems is a two-dimensional array of order `(m+1)*(n+1)`. Cell `cache[i][j]` stores the `minEditDist` of substrings of s1 and s2 up to its ith character, and j[th] character respectively.

Converting Recursion to Dynamic Programming

Code 5.4 has two variables, i and j (s1 and s2 remain constant). The DP solution uses a two-dimensional array in which all possible values of the first variable are distributed along the row and all possible values of the second variable are distributed along the column.

In recursion, the first substring is from i to `s1.length-1` and second substring is from j to `s2.length-1`, and we compare the first characters of these two substrings, i.e `s1[i]` and `s2[j]` (the current substrings starts from i and j respectively). DP solution applies the logic of recursion is applied in opposite direction, therefore in DP, if we want to compare s1[i] and s2[j], the first string is the substring of s1 from 0 to i, and second is the substring of s2 from 0 to j. Let us put these ideas into practice methodically.

✓ *Choice of tabulation*

If s1 has n characters and s2 has m characters, the total number of possible ways of picking substrings of s1 and s2 are (m+1)*(n+1). A two-dimensional array is a natural choice for storing intermediate results. Following figure shows the array for Strings "SUNDAY" and "SATURDAY".

Each cell represents the minimum edit distance between corresponding substrings. For example, Cell marked as C_{ij} in the above figure will store minimum edit distance between "SATU" and "SUN". When all the cells are filled in, the final result will be in the bottom-right cell, which will contain the minimum edit distance between "SATURDAY" and "SUNDAY".

Another reason we're using a two-dimensional array in this DP solution is that the memorised solution used a two-dimensional array as cache in the previous section. The most common application of memoization is to determine the data structure to be used in DP.

✓ *Opposite direction of Logic*

In Code 5.4, the recursive solution compares the first characters of the two substrings. We will compare the last characters of the two substrings because the direction of logic in DP is opposite to that of recursion. If the two substrings are "SATU" and "SUN", compare their last characters, which are 'U' and 'N' respectively.

✓ *Converting terminating condition to initialization*

In Code 5.4, the recursion ends when either of the two substrings is empty

111

(having zero characters). In DP, the first row is the minimum edit distance when the second substring is empty, and the leftmost column is the minimum edit distance when the first substring is empty. Initialize the first row and leftmost column based on the recursion's terminating conditions:

		S	A	T	U	R	D	A	Y
	0	1	2	3	4	5	6	7	8
S	1								
U	2								
N	3								
D	4								
A	5								
Y	6								

When one string is empty, the minimum edit distance is the number of characters in the second string.

✓ **Use same logic in opposite direction**

Fill the rest of the array using the logic of recursion beginning from the (1,1) and working row-wise till the bottom-right. Compare the corresponding characters and decide as per the logic of recursion.

In recursion, we compared the first characters of two substrings, and the logic continues (ignoring either one or both of the first characters). In DP, the logic will be applied in the opposite direction, and the last characters of the current substrings will be compared. For example, if the substrings are SATU and SUN (as shown in the diagram), compare their last characters (U and N) and use following recursion logic to ignore either one or both characters,

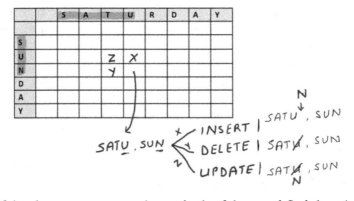

- If the characters are same, ignore both of them and find the minimum edit distance between SAT and SU, which is the value in cell **Z** above.

- If the characters are different (as in this case), there are three options:

i. **Insert** the last character of the second substring at the end of the first. The first substrings will become SATUN. The last characters of two substrings are the same now and the problem reduces to finding the minimum edit distance between SATU and SU, which is the value in cell **X**.

ii. **Delete** the last character of the first substring. The problem will then reduces to finding the minimum edit distance between SAT and SUN, which is the value in cell **Y**.

iii. **Update** the last character of the first substring and make it equal to the last character of the second substring. The two substrings become SATN and SUN. Their last characters are same, the problem now reduces to finding the minimum edit distance between SAT and SU, which is the value in cell **Z**.

Following is the logic to populate the array (except for the first row and first column, which are already initialized using the terminating condition of recursion).

$$
\texttt{EditD[i][j]} =
\begin{cases}
\texttt{EditD[i-1][j-1]} & \texttt{str1[i-1] == str2[j-1]} \\[2ex]
\texttt{1+min} \begin{bmatrix} \texttt{EditD[i-1][j]} \\ \texttt{EditD[i][j-1]} \\ \texttt{EditD[i-1][j-1]} \end{bmatrix} & \texttt{str1[i-1] != str2[j-1]}
\end{cases}
$$

Code 5.5 is the complete DP solution of above problem:

```
int editDistDP(char[] s1, char[] s2){
    int m = s1.length;
    int n = s2.length;
    int[][] editD = new int[m+1][n+1];

    for(int j=0; j<=n; j++)    // INITIALIZING 1ST ROW
        editD[0][j] = j;
    for(int i=1; i<=m; i++) // INITIALIZING 1ST COLUMN
        editD[i][0] = i;

    for (int i=1; i<=m; i++){
        for (int j=1; j<=n; j++){
            if (s1[i-1] == s2[j-1])
                editD[i][j] = editD[i-1][j-1];
```

```
    else
      editD[i][j] = getMinimum(editD[i][j-1],
                               editD[i-1][j],
                               editD[i-1][j-1]) + 1;
    }
  }
  return editD[m][n];
}
```

Code: 5.5

Code 5.5 will populate the matrix as below for input strings "SUNDAY" and "SATURDAY". The minimum edit distance is 3.

		S	A	T	U	R	D	A	Y
	0	1	2	3	4	5	6	7	8
S	1	0	1	2	3	4	5	6	7
U	2	1	1	2	2	3	4	5	6
N	3	2	2	2	3	3	4	5	6
D	4	3	3	3	3	4	3	4	5
A	5	4	3	4	4	4	4	3	4
Y	6	5	4	4	5	5	5	4	3

Also note that the Minimum-Edit-Distance operation is commutative.

Example 5.3: Modify the solution of Example 5.2 to print the operations instead of finding the minimum number of operations.

Solution: After populating the array using the logic in Code 5.5, backtrack the solution from the bottom-right corner to the top-left corner using the same logic. When moving diagonally up, if the corresponding characters as the same, they are not changed; otherwise follow the path of minimum value out of the three options and apply the operations accordingly.

Following is the code to print minimum number of operations that need to be performed on s1 to make it equal to s2.

```
void printOps(int[][] editD, char[] s1, char[] s2){
  int m = editD.length - 1; // LAST ROW
  int n = editD[0].length - 1; // LAST COL

  while(m>0 || n>0){
    if(s1[m-1] == s2[n-1]){
      m--; n--;
    }else{
      if(n == 0){
        System.out.println("DELETE "+s1[m-1]);
        m--;
      } else if(m == 0){
        System.out.println("DELETE "+s2[n-1]);
        n--;
      } else {
        int min = getMinimum(editD[m][n-1],
                             editD[m-1][n],
                             editD[m-1][n-1] );
        if(min == editD[m-1][n]) {
          System.out.println("DELETE "+s1[m-1]);
          m--;
        }else if(min == editD[m][n-1]){
          System.out.println("INSERT "+s2[n-1]);
          n--;
        }else{
          System.out.println("UPDATE "+s1[m-1]);
          m--; n--;
        }
      }
    }
  }
}
```

Code: 5.6

Code 5.6 takes O(m*n). But this prints just one minimum edit distance operations. There may be more than one set of operations, all resulting in minimum edit distance. For example, minimum edit distance between **AB** and **X**, is 2, and there are following two ways to get that,

    i.   Update the first character to **X** and delete the second character.

    ii.   Update the second character to **X** and delete the first character.

Following will the array of Code 5.5 for these two strings,

		A	B
	0	1	2
X	1	1	2

There are two ways in which we can backtrack from the bottom-right cell,

		A	B
	0	1	2
X	1	1	2

The two ways indicate that there are two options for the last character (**B**), either delete it or update it to the corresponding character (**X**). If you choose to delete it, then in the next step you have to update the next character (**A**), and if you choose to update **B** then next step is to delete **A**.

		A	B
	0	1	2
X	1	1	2

		A	B
	0	1	2
X	1	1	2

If interviewer want you to print all possible outputs, you have to scan all possible paths of minimum edit distance. The logic of this is similar to finding all root-to-leaf paths in a binary tree, just that in this case we will start from the bottom-left and call the recursion for each of the minimum paths. In the worst case there may be three recursive calls at each step(when all the three values are same).

Example 5.4 (String Interleaving): String **C** is said to be interleaving of two strings **A** and **B** if it contains all and only the characters from **A** and **B** and maintains the relative order of these characters in both the strings. In the following example, C is interleaving of A and B.

```
A = "xyz"
B = "abcd"
C = "xabyczd"
```

string **C** is the interleaving of strings **A** and **B** as shown in following diagram:

Write a function that accepts three strings and checks if the third string is the interleaving of the first and second strings.

Recursive Solution

An obvious check is that if the length of the third string is not equal to the sum of the lengths of the first two strings, then the result is false.

As in the previous example, the core logic will check one character (current index) from the three strings. Initially all the indexes are 0. Let us assume that the current index of **A** is i, **B** is j and **C** is k. For the current character of **C**, i.e **C[k]**, there are following possibilities:

i.   **C[k]** is neither equal **A[i]** nor equal to **B[j]**. Terminate the recursion and return `false` because **C** cannot be the interleaving of **A** and **B**.

ii.   **C[k]** is equal to **A[i]** but not equal to **B[j]**. It implies that **C[k]** must have come from **A[i]**. The problem now reduces to checking if substrings of **A** and **B** starting from (i+1) and j respectively, interleave to form substring of **C** starting from index (k+1).

iii.   **C[k]** is equal to **B[j]** but not equal to **A[i]**. It implies that **C[k]** must have come from **B[j]**. The problem now reduces to checking if substrings of **A** and **B** starting from i and (j+1) respectively, interleave to form substring of **C** starting from index (k+1).

iv.   **C[k]** is equal to both **A[i]** and **B[j]** (all three of them are same). In this case **C[k]** can come either from **A[i]** or **B[j]**. There are two options, and each option results in separate recursion (either point ii. or iii. above). Explore both the options and return `true` if anyone of them returns `true`.

Consider the same three strings again,
A = "xyz"   B = "abcd"   C = "xabyczd"

The first character **x** of **C** obviously comes from string **A**, because the first character of **B** is not **x**.

The problem now reduces to checking if string "abyczd" is an interleaving of strings "yz" and "abcd". i.e
A = "yz"   B = "abcd"   C = "xabyczd"

This problem is of the same type as the original problem and can be solved recursively.

Another example can be when the first character of both **A** and **B** are same, which is also same as the first character of C, as in the below example:
A = "bcc"   B = "bbca"   C = "bbcbcac"

In this case **C[0]** can either come from **A** or from **B**. No greedy approach will work for this problem and we have to explore both the possibilities of **C[0]** to be taken from either **A[0]** or **B[0]**.

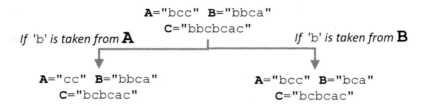

In both the cases the problem is reduced to sub problems of the same type that can be solved recursively. Extending the above function call tree reveals overlapping subproblems as shown below.

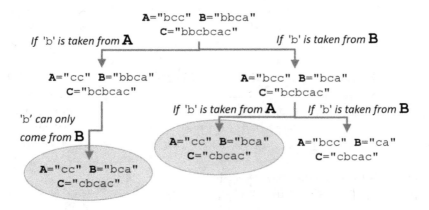

The two subproblems inside circles are the same, and this subproblem is solved twice during the computation of the main problem's solution. If the strings are long, there may be a lot of overlapping subproblems.

Following recursive function accept three strings **A**, **B** and **C** and returns true if string **C** is interleaving of strings **A** and **B**. **i**, **j** and **k** are the indices of current characters in the three strings respectively,

```
boolean isInterleaving(char[] A, char[] B, char[] C,
                       int i, int j, int k){
  // IF STRINGS ARE EMPTY
  if(i == A.length && j == B.length && k == C.length)
    return true;

  // EITHER C IS EMPTY OR BOTH A & B BOTH ARE EMPTY
  if( (k==C.length) || (i==A.length && j==B.length))
    return false;

  boolean res1 = false;
  boolean res2 = false;

  // IF CURRENT CHAR OF A = CURRENT CHAR OF C
  if(i<A.length && A[i] == C[k])
    res1 = isInterleaving(A, B, C, i+1, j, k+1);

  // IF CURRENT CHAR OF B = CURRENT CHAR OF C
  if(res1 == false && (j<B.length && B[j] == C[k]) )
    res2 = isInterleaving(A, B, C, i, j+1, k+1);

  return (res1 || res2);
}
```

Code: 5.7

Converting Recursion to Dynamic Programming

This problem's tabulation is very similar to the tabulation of previous two-variable problem in Example 5.2. There are two Strings (the third string is a result against which we check our values), and at any point, we will look at the first **x** characters of string **A** and first **y** characters from string **B** to see if they interleave to form the first **x+y** characters of string **C**. Please note that the number of characters in C is fixed, i.e **x+y**. The recursive function in Code 5.7 may give an impression that there are three variables, but there are only two.

Choice of tabulation

Use a two-dimensional array with string **A** along one dimension and **B** along the other. Cell (**i,j**) indicates whether or not first **i** characters of **A** and first **j** characters of **B** interleave to form first (**i+j**) characters of **C**. Please note again that the number of characters in the substring of **C** are always equal to the sum of number of characters in the substrings of **A** and **B**.

For example, cell (2,3) represents if "bc" (first 2 characters of "bcc") and "bbc" (first 3 characters of string "bbca") interleave to form "bbcbc" (first 5 characters of string "bbcbcac") or not. In our solution this should be true because "bc" and "bbc" can interleave to form "bbcbc".

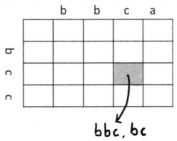

bbc, bc

Opposite direction of Logic

Because recursion in Code 5.7 was comparing the first characters in two substrings, the DP solution should compares the last characters of current substrings.

Converting terminating condition to initialization

Populate the first row and first column using the terminating conditions of recursion. The value of cell (0,0) should be true. It means that if all of the strings are of lengths zero, the answer is true, which is the first terminating condition of recursion in Code 5.7.

	b	b	c	a
T				

First row means that substring of **A** is empty. In this case, we should check only the second substring. Effectively it will just check if substring of **B** is same as that of substring of **C**:

```
IF (B[i] != C[i])
    MAT[0][i] = FALSE
ELSE
    MAT[0][i] = MAT[0][i-1]
```

Similarly, the first column is populated using the following logic,

```
IF (A[j] != C[j])
    MAT[j][0] = FALSE
ELSEs
    MAT[j][0] = MAT[j-1][0]
```

After initializing the first row and the first column the array will look like:

		b	b	c	a
	T	T	T	T	F
b	T				
c	F				
c	F				

✓   ***Use same logic in opposite direction***

For rest of the cells there are four possibilities

    i. Current character of substring of **C** is neither equal to current character of substring of **A** nor of **B**.

    ii. Current character of substring **C** is equal to current character of substring of **A** but not of **B**.

    iii. Current character of substring of **C** is equal to current character of substring of **B**, but not of **A**.

    iv. Current character of substring of **C** is equal to current characters of substrings of both **A** and **B** (all three are same).

All of these possibilities are handled using the logic already discussed earlier in recursion. Following is the code of DP.

```
boolean isInterleaving(char[] A, char[] B, char[] C){
    int M = A.length;
    int N = B.length;

    if(C.length != M+N)
        return false;
```

```
boolean[][] Mat = new boolean[M+1][N+1];

// INITIALIZATION
Mat[0][0] = true;
for(int i=1; i<=M; i++){          // FIRST COL
   if(A[i-1] != C[i-1])
     Mat[i][0] = false;
   else
     Mat[i][0] = Mat[i-1][0];
}
for(int j=1; j<=N; j++){          // FIRST ROW
   if(B[j-1] != C[j-1])
     Mat[0][j] = false;
   else
     Mat[0][j] = Mat[0][j-1];
}

for (int i=1; i<=M; ++i){
   for (int j=1; j<=N; ++j){
     // CURRENT CHAR OF C SAME AS A BUT NOT B
     if( A[i-1]==C[i+j-1] && B[j-1]!=C[i+j-1] )
       Mat[i][j] = Mat[i-1][j];

     // CURRENT CHAR OF C SAME AS B BUT NOT A
     else if(A[i-1]!=C[i+j-1] && B[j-1]==C[i+j-1])
       Mat[i][j] = Mat[i][j-1];

     // CURRENT CHAR OF C SAME AS BOTH A AND B
     else if( A[i-1]==C[i+j-1] && B[j-1]==C[i+j-1])
       Mat[i][j]=(Mat[i-1][j] || Mat[i][j-1]);

     // CURRENT CHAR OF C NEITHER FROM A NOR B
     else
       Mat[i][j] = false;
   }
}

return Mat[M][N];
}
```

Code: 5.8

This DP solution takes polynomial time, $O(m*n)$ as opposed to the exponential time taken by recursion. For input strings, bbca, bcc and bbcbcac, Code 5.8 will populate the array as follows. The value stored in the bottom-right cell is the final answer.

	b	b	c	a
	T	T	T	T	F
σ	T	T	F	T	F
∩	F	T	T	T	T
∩	F	F	T	F	T

C = b b c b c a c

Question 5.1: Given two strings, print all possible interleavings of these strings. For example,

```
INPUT: "AB" "XY"
OUTPUT: ABXY AXBY AXYB XABY XAYB XYAB
```

Question 5.2: In Example 5.3, if all the characters in String A are different from those in String B, do we still need the 2-dim array? Suggest a $O(n+m)$ time algorithm that takes $O(1)$ extra memory and gives the result for this particular case when two strings does not have any common character.

Example 5.5 (Longest Common Subsequence): Find the number of characters in the Longest Common Subsequence (LCS) of two given strings. The LCS of "ABCD" and "AEBD", is "ABD" of length 3.

A subsequence of a string **S**, is a sub set of characters from **S** in the same relative order as in **S**. For example,

- ACT , ATTC , T , ACTTGC are all subsequence of ACTTGCG,
- TTA is not a subsequence of string ACTTGCG.

A string of length n has 2^n subsequences(including the null sequence and the full string[10]).

A **common subsequence** of two strings is a sequence of characters which is subsequence of both the strings. A longest common subsequence (LCS) is the maximum length common subsequence of two strings. If S1 and S2 are following two strings:

```
S1 = AAACCGTGAGTTATTCGTTCTAGAA
S2 = CACCCCTAAGGTACCTTTGGTTC
```

---

[10] There are two choices for each character of the string, include it in the subsequence or not. Each choice will result in a different subsequences at each element.

Their LCS is ACCTAGTACTTTG which is present in both:

```
S1 = AAACCGTGAGTTATTCGTTCTAGAA
S2 = CACCCCTAAGGTACCTTTGGTTC
```

Recursive Solution

The recursion involving an array, string, or list data structure begins by processing either the first or last characters of each. In any case, the goal is to reduce the size of list for the next recursion. Begin by comparing the first characters of these two strings. At any point, let i and j be the current indices of the two strings.

The signature of function is very important in recursion.

```
int lcs(char[] s1, char[] s2, int i, int j)
```

The function finds the LCS between substring of s1 and s2 starting from index i of s1 and index j of s2 till the end of two strings. Compare the first characters of the two substrings. There are two possibilities:

1. **Both are same (**s1[i] = s2[j]**)**
   This character is part of the longest common subsequence (LCS). It means we have already found one character in LCS. Find the LCS of substrings of s1 and s2 starting from index (i+1) of s1 and index (j+1) of s2 till the end of two strings and add one (for current character) to this LCS.

2. **Both are different (**s1[i] != s2[j]**)**
   Both characters cannot be part of the LCS at the same time. Make two recursive calls, one including s1[i] but excluding s2[j] and other excluding s1[i] and including s2[j] and return the maximum of two values.

Case 1:

```
LCS("ABCD", "AEBD") = 1 + LCS("BCD", "EBD")
```

Case 2:

```
LCS("EABCD", "FAEBD") = Max( LCS("EABCD", "AEBD"),
                             LCS("ABCD", "FAEBD"))
```

Following code in java converts this logic to code.

```
int lcs(char[] s1, char[] s2, int i, int j){
  // TERMINATING CONDITION
```

```
if (i == s1.length || j == s2.length)
    return 0;

// COMPARING CURRENT CHARACTERS
if (s1[i] == s2[j])
    return 1 + lcs(s1, s2, i+1, j+1);
else
    return getMax( lcs(s1, s2, i+1, j),
                   lcs(s1, s2, i, j+1));
}
```

Code: 5.9

getMax returns maximum of two integer values as defined below:
```
int getMax(int x, int y){
    return (x > y)? x : y;
}
```

In the worst case, when all the characters in the two strings are different, code 5.9 takes $O(2^n)$ time because every function calls itself twice, as shown in the following function call diagram:

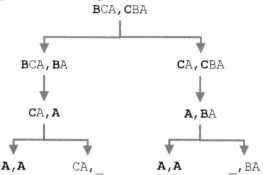

As shown in the diagram above, the recursive solution has optimal substructure and overlapping subproblems.

Memoization

Take a two dimensional array, of size $(m+1) * (n+1)$ as cache.
```
int[][] cache = new int[m+1][n+1];
```

Store the LCS of first **i** characters of **X** and **j** characters of **Y** in cell cache[i][j]. (Equally we may choose to store the LCS of remaining **i** characters of **X** and remaining **j** characters of **Y** in this cell). In any case, a

125

subproblem is solved only once and a direct lookup of the solution happens the next time we encounter that subproblem. The following code takes $O(m*n)$ time. It assumes all the cells in cache are initialized to -1.

```
int lcs(int[][] cache, char[] s1, char[] s2,
                                 int i, int j ){
  // TERMINATING CONDITION
  if (i == s1.length || j == s2.length)
    return 0;

  // VALUE ALREADY COMPUTED
  if(cache[i][j] != -1)
    return cache[i][j];

  // COMPUTING THE VALUE FOR THE FIRST TIME
  if (s1[i] == s2[j])
    cache[i][j] = 1 + lcs(table, s1, s2, i+1, j+1);
  else
    cache[i][j] = getMax( lcs(table, s1, s2, i, j+1),
                   lcs(table, s1, s2, i+1, j));

  return cache[i][j];
}
```

Code: 5.10

Converting Recursion to Dynamic Programming

The bottom-up DP solution populates the table with length of LCS of the sub-strings of given strings building on to the final solution.

Choice of tabulation

As in previous examples, use a two-dimensional array and place one string along the row and the other string along the column, as shown in the diagram for strings "ABCD" and "AEBD".

	φ	A	E	B	D
φ	0	0	0	0	0
A	0				
B	0				
C	0				
D	0				

Converting terminating condition to initialization

The first row represents the case when the second string is empty, and the first column represents the case when the first string is empty. In both cases, the length of LCS is 0.

Using same logic in opposite direction

Start populating the array in row-wise order using the following logic of recursion:

```
IF (s1[i-1] == s2[j-1])
   LCSCnt[i][j] = LCSCnt[i-1][j-1] + 1;
ELSE
   LCSCnt[i][j] = max(LCSCnt[i-1][j], LCSCnt[i][j-1]);
```

The following array shows the values and the final result is in its bottom-right cell.

	φ	A	E	B	D
φ	0	0	0	0	0
A	0	1	1	1	1
B	0	1	1	2	2
C	0	1	1	2	2
D	0	1	1	2	3

```
int lcs(char[] s1, char[] s2){
  int m = s1.length;
  int n = s2.length;
  int[][] lcsCnt = new int[m+1][n+1];

  // INITIALIZATION
  for(int i=0; i<=m; i++)
    lcsCnt[i][0] = 0;
  for(int i=0; i<=n; i++)
    lcsCnt[0][i] = 0;

  for(int i=1; i<=m; i++){
    for(int j=1; j<=n; j++){
      if (s1[i-1] == s2[j-1])
        lcsCnt[i][j] = lcsCnt[i-1][j-1] + 1;
      else
        lcsCnt[i][j] = getMax(lcsCnt[i-1][j],
```

```
                              lcsCnt[i][j-1] );
    }
  }
  return lcsCnt[m][n];
}
```

Code: 5.11

Example 5.6: Extend the solution of previous example to also print a longest common subsequence. For example, the output of the previous example should be "ABD" (If there are more than one LCSs, you can print any of those LCSs).

Solution: Fill the array with Code 5.11 first, then backtrack from the bottom-right corner of the array and print either one or all the longest common subsequences.

If we remember where the value of each cell comes from while filling the lcsCnt matrix, the value is either:

1. Same as the cell on left side of current cell, or
2. Same as the cell above the current cell, or
3. 1 + the value of cell on left-upper diagonal of current cell.

Out of the above three points, we need to keep a special note of point 3. It happens when the current character of both the strings is part of the LCS. In the following diagram, there is a diagonal movement for character A, B and D. Hence the LCS is ABD:

	φ	A	E	B	D
φ	0	0	0	0	0
A	0	1	1	1	1
B	0	1	1	2	2
C	0	1	1	2	2
D	0	1	1	2	3

We just need to trace back from the bottom-right cell and trace the path till the top row or leftmost column. While backtracking ignore everything, except for the diagonal movements.

Whenever there is a diagonal movement, add the corresponding character to the head of the list that holds the LCS. The LCS in the following diagram is **ABD**.

	Φ	A	E	B	D
Φ	0	0	0	0	0
A	0	1	1	1	1
B	0	1	1	2	2
C	0	1	1	2	2
D	0	1	1	2	3

If matrix `lcsCnt` is defined globally and is already populated by the `lcs` function of Code 5.11. The code for printing the longest common subsequence from this array is as follows:

```
String getLCS(char[] s1, char[] s2){
   int m = s1.length;
   int n = s2.length;

   int[][] lcsCnt = lcs(s1, s2);
   String lcs = new String();
   int i = m, j = n;

   // Continue till we hit the top or left wall
   while (i > 0 && j > 0){
     if (s1[i-1] == s2[j-1]){
        lcs = s1[i-1] + lcs;
        i--;
        j--;
        idx--;
     } else if (lcsCnt[i-1][j] > lcsCnt[i][j-1]){
        i--;
     } else{
        j--;
     }
   }

   return lcs;
}
```
Code: 5.12

Note that Code 5.12 is a greedy code that returns only one LCS. If two strings have more than one Longest common subsequences, it will return only one of them. If the two values `lcsCnt[i-1][j]` and `lcsCnt[i][j-1]` are equal, there are two possible paths at this point resulting in two different LCSs. Similarly, at any point there may be two different ways to go.

If interviewer want you to find all possible LCSs of two strings, then you must trace all these possible paths backward. The logic of this is similar to the logic of finding all root-to-leaf paths in a binary tree, or finding all possible minimum edit distances between two strings discussed in the previous section.

Question 5.3: Given an array of integers, write code that returns the length of the longest increasing subsequence in that array. For example, the longest increasing subsequence of array,
`{3, 1, 6, 2, 4, 0, 5}`

is of length 4 (the longest increasing subsequence is `{1, 2, 4, 5}`).

Question 5.4: In question 5.3, how will you print the longest increasing subsequence of the array?

Question 5.5: A sequence is bitonic if it first monotonically increases and then monotonically decreases. For example the sequences (1, 4, 6, 8, 3, −2) , (9, 2, −4, −10, −5) , and (1, 2, 3, 4) are all bitonic, but (1, 3, 12, 4, 2, 10) is not bitonic.

Write a function that accepts an array of integers and returns the length of longest bitonic subsequence of the array.

Please note that a sequence sorted in increasing order is bitonic with empty decreasing part and similarly a sequence in decreasing order is bitonic with empty increasing part.

Hint: A bitonic sequence can be circularly shifted to monotonically increase (or monotonically decrease sequence).

Question 5.6: Change the above question to print the longest bitonic subsequence of an array.

Question 5.7: Given an integer n, and an array of integers, `arr` holding the indices (0<=`arr.length`<n). Find the number of valid expressions of length 2n having n pairs of valid parentheses. For example, if n=3, and `arr = {1}` then the output should be 3 because there are 3 proper possible ways of having three pairs of valid parentheses,
`(())()`   `((()))`   `(()())`

In all the three cases, the parenthesis at index 1 is an open parenthesis.

Example 5.6 (Shortest Common Supersequence): Given two strings s1 and s2, find the length of the shortest string that has both s1 and s2 as subsequences. For example, the shortest common supersequence between the following two strings,
```
S1 = "XYXZ"
S2 = "ZXY"
```

Is ZXYXZ and is of length 5.

This problem has a step-by-step similarity with the Longest common subsequence problem discussed in Example 5.5.

There are two possibilities for the current characters of s1 and s2,

1. **Both are same (s1[i] = s2[j])**
   This character is part of the shortest common supersequence (SCS). Find the SCS of substrings of s1 and s2 starting from index (i+1) of s1 and index (j+1) of s2 till the end of two strings and add one (for current character) to this SCS.

2. **Both are different (s1[i] != s2[j])**
   Both characters need to be part of the SCS. But, whether we should put s1[i] first or s2[j], we do not know. Make two recursive calls, one including s1[i] in the result and finding the SCS of s1 and s2 starting from (i+1) and j respectively. And the other including s2[j] in the result and finding the SCS of s1 and s2 starting from i and j+1 respectively. Return the minimum of the two options.

Following is the code for recursive solution:
```
int scs(char[] s1, char[] s2, int i, int j){
  if(i >= s1.length){ return s2.length - j; }
  if(j >= s2.length){ return s1.length - i; }

  if(s1[i] == s2[j])
    return 1 + scs(s1, s2, i+1, j+1);

  int a = 1 + scs(s1, s2, i+1, j);
  int b = 1 + scs(s1, s2, i, j+1);

  return getMin(a, b);
}
```

Question 5.8: Write the recursive solution to return the string of Shortest common supersequence.

Question 5.9: Convert the recursion in Example 5.6 to DP to find the length of SCS in polynomial time.

Question 5.10: Convert the recursion in Question 5.8 to DP to find a SCS string in polynomial time. How will change this solution to find all the strings representing SCS.

6

Considering all options for each element

Majority of Dynamic Programming problems are optimization problems. In the next chapter, we will see that the most fundamental difference between Greedy and DP is that DP considers all possible solutions and then pick the most optimal one out of them, whereas Greedy takes the most intuitive approach and develops the solution based on one intuition. Because DP solutions find all possible solutions, it should consider every possible permutation of the variables in the problem.

Recursion is central to DP. The logic of recursion picks one element (usually the first element) from the collection, considers all possible values for that element, and then, for each value, passes the rest of the collection (minus this element) to the recursion. Bottom-up Dynamic Programming also employs this logic of recursion. So, while DP considers all possible elements, our primary focus is on considering the possibilities of one element at a time.

Example 4.1 considers all possible cells from where you may reach the current cell in one step. Similarly, Example 5.1 also considers all options of making the first cut in an iron rod of length n.

This chapter examines DP problems where the 'consider-all-possibilities-for-each-element' component is dominant. This first section discusses problems with only two options per element. Usually, the option is to either include or exclude that element from the result. Problems with each element having multiple options are discussed in the second part of this chapter.

As said earlier also, these problem categories are not mutually exclusive. There could be an include-exclude logic in the path problem also. Similarly, a path problem may be approached as a two-variable problem. So, remember what we have already discussed in previous chapters as you solve problems in this (and subsequent) chapter.

Two Options (Include-Exclude Options)

While solving some DP problems, you may come across a situation where, for each element in the problem, you have two options,

    i.   Include this element in the result, or
    ii.   Exclude this element from the result.

Each option produces a distinct subproblem that lead to a separate path which can be delegated to recursion, with each instance of the function dealing with only what needs to be done before or after the recursion. Most of the problems discussed here can be mapped to the CNF Satisfiability Problem.

Example 6.1 (Subset Sum): Given an array of non-negative integers and a number X, determine if there exist a subset of elements of the array with sum equal to X. For example:

Input Array: {3, 2, 7, 1} **X** = 6
Output: True (because sum of (3, 2, 1) is 6)

Recursion

The recursive solution of this problem is relatively easy, at each element, there are two possibilities,

1. Include the element in the sum, or
2. Do not include the element in the sum.

If the input array is {3, 2, 7, 1}, and X=6, the first element (i.e. 3) can be included or excluded from the subset. When 3 is included in the subset, the problem reduces to determining whether a subset with sum = X−3 exists in the remaining array. If you decide not to include 3 in the subset, you must find whether a subset with sum = X exists in the remaining array.

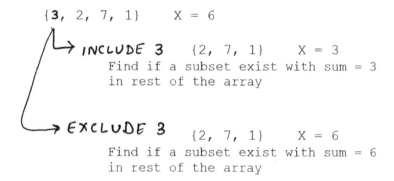

{3, 2, 7, 1}   X = 6

INCLUDE 3   {2, 7, 1}   X = 3
Find if a subset exist with sum = 3
in rest of the array

EXCLUDE 3   {2, 7, 1}   X = 6
Find if a subset exist with sum = 6
in rest of the array

In both cases, we are left with a similar type of problem that can be solved using recursion. The recursion terminates when either X becomes 0 (success) or the array is exhausted (fail). The recursive solution is shown in the following code.

```
boolean subsetSum(int[] a, int i, int X){
  if(X == 0)
    return true;

  if(i == a.length) // REACHED END OF ARRAY
    return false;

  // IF EXCLUDE IS THE ONLY OPTION
  if (a[i] > X)
    return subsetSum (a, i+1, X);

  return   subsetSum(a, i+1, X) ||
           subsetSum(a, i+1, X-a[i]);
}
```

Clearly, the subproblems are overlapping, and this solution is taking exponential time, i.e. $O(2^n)$.

Memoization

Memoization cache the results of subproblems. There are two parameters in the recursive solution, starting index of the array, and X. A two-dimensional array can be used as a cache where we can put the index of array along one dimension and all possible values of X (from 0 to X) along the other dimension. cache[i][j] will be true if there exists a subset of first i elements of the array with sum = j. The final result will be in the bottom-right cell, cache[a.length][X].

The Dynamic Programming Solution discussed below, also use the same matrix and populate it using the logic of recursion.

Dynamic Programming Solution

DP solves the problem bottom-up, storing the intermediate results in a matrix MAT. MAT[i][j] is true if there is a subset of arr[0 .. j-1] with sum equal to i, otherwise it is false. The final value will be in cell MAT[X][arr.length].

If input array is {3, 2, 7, 1} and X is 6, the matrix MAT will be of size 5*7. Column of matrix goes from 0 to X and rows for elements of the array as shown in the following diagram:

	0	1	2	3	4	5	6
Array has 0 elements { }	1	0	0	0	0	0	0
Array has 1 element {3}	1	0	0	1	0	0	0
Array has 2 elements {3,2}	1	0	1	1	0	1	0
Array has 3 elements {3,2,7}	1	0	1	1	0	1	0
Array has 4 elements {3,2,7,1}	1	1	1	1	1	1	1

The current subarray (section of the array under consideration) is initially empty (in row 0). In each subsequent row, we add a new value to the current subarray, and that value is the value considered for that row. The value for the second row is 3, value for third row is 2, and so on. Another way to look at it is that in the DP solution, the include-exclude logic is applied to the last element of the subarray because indexes in recursion are considered in forward order beginning with index-0.

Using the first terminating condition of recursion, set all the cells of the first column to true because if X is 0 then the answer is zero. Similarly, the entire first row is false (except for first cell where X=0), because if array does not have any elements, then it can't have a subset with non-zero sum.

	0	1	2	3	4	5	6
{}	T	F	F	F	F	F	F
{3}	T						
{3,2}	T						
{3,2,7}	T						
{3,2,7,1}	T						

Element for the next row is 3. Either include 3 in the subset or exclude 3 from the subset (in which case the subset will be empty). With only one 3, we can only have the sum as 3 and nothing else (for 6 we need two 3's, but we just have one). For the first 3 columns in the second row, excluding 3 is the only option because you cannot get a sum of 0, 1, or 2 by including 3. Following that, there are two options, and the result will be true if either of them is true. `a[i][j] = (a[i-1][j-3] || a[i-1][j])`

	0	1	2	3	4	5	6
{}	T	F	F	F	F	F	F
{3}	T	F	F	T	F	F	F
{3,2}	T						
{3,2,7}	T						
{3,2,7,1}	T						

Fill the matrix in row-wise order (starting with the second row). While populating the ith row, if **v** is the element of that row (ex. **v** for row-1 is 3, for row-2 is 2, for row-3 is 7, and row-4 is 1), the first **v** positions in the row will be exact copy from the cell above it in the i-1 row because excluding **v** is the only option.

	0	1	2	3	4	5	6
{}	T	F	F	F	F	F	F
{3}	T	F	F	T	F	F	F
{3,2}	T	F					
{3,2,7}	T						
{3,2,7,1}	T						

For all other columns, again look in the row above it:

- **IF** value in cell (i-1, j) is True then cell (i, j) is also True.
- **ELSE**, look in the cell (i-1, j-**v**), and copy the content of cell (i-1, j-v) to cell (i,j).

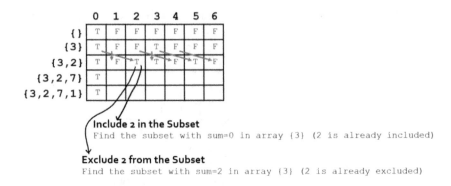

Include 2 in the Subset
Find the subset with sum=0 in array {3} (2 is already included)

Exclude 2 from the Subset
Find the subset with sum=2 in array {3} (2 is already excluded)

Perform Logical-OR of values in cells (i-1,j) and (i-1,j-v). This logic is coming straight from the recursive solution. After filling all the values, the matrix will look like below

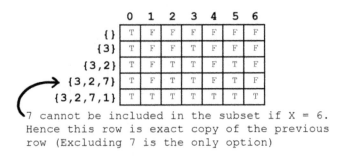

7 cannot be included in the subset if X = 6.
Hence this row is exact copy of the previous
row (Excluding 7 is the only option)

The final solution is the value in the bottom-right cell of the matrix.

```
boolean isSubarrSum(int[] a, int X){
  boolean[][] MAT = new boolean[a.length+1][X+1];

  // USE TERMINATING COND. OF RECURSIO TO INITIALIZE
  for (int i = 0; i <= a.length; i++)
    MAT[i][0] = true;

  for(int i=1; i<=a.length; i++)
    MAT[0][i] = false;

  // Fill MAT botton up using logic of recursion
  for(int i=1; i<=a.length; i++){
    for(int j=1; j<=X; j++){
      MAT[i][j] = MAT[i-1][j];
      if (j >= a[i-1])
        MAT[i][j] = MAT[i-1][j] || MAT[i-1][j-a[i-1]];
    }
  }
```

```
        return MAT[a.length][X];
}
```

This DP solution takes polynomial time $= O(m.n)$ equal to the dimension of the matrix.

Question 6.1: Given an array of numbers and a number X, find if a pair (**two** numbers) exist in the array with sum=X.

This question is not dynamic programming problem. There are multiple solutions to this problem, including a linear time solution that takes O(n) time and O(n) extra memory.[11]

Question 6.2: Example 6.1 is returning a boolean value indicating whether or not a subset exist with the given sum. It is not actually returning (or printing) that subset. For example, if array is {3, 2, 7, 1} and X is 6, the function will return true, but it will not print the subset (3, 2, 1). Change the DP solution to also return the subset.

Example 6.2 (Equal sum partition): Determine whether you can partition elements of an array of non-negative integers into two subsets such that the sum of values in these two is equal. If such a division exist, return true; otherwise, false.

Input Array: {1, 5, 11, 5, 4, 2}
Output: True. The given array can be partitioned as {5, 5, 4} and {1, 11, 2}.

One way of solving this problem is by using the subset sum solution given in Example 6.1 using the following steps:

   i. Find the sum of all the elements in the array.
   ii. If the sum is odd, return False, because there can not be two subsets with equal sum, so return false.
   iii. If sum of array elements is even, find if there exist a subset with sum equal to half of the total sum of all the array elements.

---

[11] It is discussed in our book, "Searching and Sorting for Coding Interviews".

Or we can develop a completely new recursion independent of Example 6.1 and then optimize that recursion using DP.

Recursion

Start with two empty sets, Set-1 and Set-2. Traverse the given array, for each element of the array there are two options. It can either goes to Set-1, or to Set-2. Both of these options will produce two distinct recursions. Finally, if the sum of elements in the two sets is the same, return true; otherwise, return false.

Instead of two sets, we can just keep two variables representing the sum of two sets because we want to compute the sum of elements and return a boolean value. If the question is to also return the set, maintain the sets.

```
boolean canPartition(int[] a, int i, int s1, int s2){
  if(i == a.length)
    return (s1 == s2);

  boolean x = canPartition(a, i+1, s1+a[i], s2);
  boolean y = canPartition(a, i+1, s1, s2+a[i]);

  return x||y;
}
```

You can use a two-dimensional array to convert the above recursion to DP.

Example 6.3 (Maximum sum non-adjacent subsequence): Given an array of non-negative numbers, find the maximum sum of a subsequence such that no two elements subsequence are adjacent in the array. For example, if the array is {3, 2, 7, 10}, then the answer should be 13 which is the sum of elements in subsequence {3, 10}.

Recursion

For every element in the array there are two choices,

1. Include the element in the subsequence.
2. Do not include the element in the subsequence.

Follow both the paths and return the maximum of two. Note that including the current element is an option only if the previous element in the array was not included.

```
static int maxSubSeqSum(int[] a, int i){
    if(i >= a.length){ return 0; }

    // INCLUDE a[i]
    int x = a[i] + maxSubSeqSum(a, i+2);

    // EXCLUDE a[i]
    int y = maxSubSeqSum(a, i+1);

    return getMax(x, y);
}
```

In the above code, if a[i] is included in the subsequence, then a[i+1] cannot be included. This function takes $O(2^n)$ time because of overlapping subproblems.

Memoization

A one-dimensional array can be used as a cache and the result for index I can be stored at cache[i].

Dynamic Programming Solution

The dynamic programming solution of this problem will use a one-dimensional array (because there is only once variable in the recursion). This array will be populated from the beginning and ith index of the array will store the max sum of subsequence of array index-i. The logic of recursion will be used to populate the array.

```
static int maxSubSeqSum(int[] a){
    if(a.length == 1){ return a[0]; }
    int[] dp = new int[a.length];
    dp[0] = a[0];
    dp[1] = getMax(a[0], a[1]);
    for(int i=2; i<a.length; i++){
```

```
    int x = a[i] + dp[i-2]; // INCLUDE a[i]
    int y = dp[i-1]; // EXCLUDE a[i]
    dp[i] = getMax(x, y);
  }


  return dp[a.length-1];
}
```

Optimizing the DP further

The DP solution is using an array. For any index in the dp array, we are only using the previous two values in that array. So, we can further optimize the solution by taking two variables instead of an array.

Question 6.3 : Given an array of integers, find the maximum sum of any non-empty subsequence of the array such that the numbers in the subsequence are in non-decreasing order. For example, if the input array is {1, 5, 2, 4, 9, 6}, then 16 which is the sum of subsequence {1, 2, 4, 9}. Note that there may be more than one increasing subsequence resulting in maximum sum.

Question 6.4: Write the logic to print the subsequence for Example 6.3.

Question 6.5: Given an array of integers, divide the numbers into two sets so that the difference between the sums of the elements in the two sets is minimum.

If input array is {7, 6, 1, 13}. Then the two subsets are {7, 6,1} and {13}. Sum of elements of first subset = 7+6+1 = 14. Sum of elements in second subset = 13. Difference between sums = 1.

Multiple options

This logic extends the Include-Exclude logic. Every element in the Include-Exclude logic had two options: include it or exclude it, but sometimes the number of options for an element is more than two. In such a case, consider each option and explore all possible options of the other elements for each option of the current element. For example, in the train fair problems discussed in Example 3.2, we looked at all possible places where a person can be just before reaching the last station. Let us take some examples,

Example 6.4 (Dice throwing): A dice has 6 faces having values 1 to 6. Given a number X, find the number of ways to get a sum of X in successive throws. For example, if X=7, then we can get 3 using following 4 ways

```
1, 1, 1    // THROW DICE 3 TIMES WITH A 1 EACH TIME
1, 2       // GET 1 IN 1st THROW, AND 2 IN 2nd THROW
2, 1       // GET 2 IN 1st THROW, AND 1 IN 2nd THROW
3          // GET 3 IN THE FRIST THROW
```

Recursion

There are 6 possible outcomes in the first throw. For each of these outcomes, there are another 6 outcomes in the second throw and so on. Stop when the required sum becomes 0 or negative. If the required sum becomes negative, then there is no way to get that output.

```
int numWays(int X){
  if(X < 0){ return 0; }
  if(X == 0){ return 1; }
  int sum = 0;
  for(int i=1; i<=6; i++){
    sum += numWays(X-i);
  }
  return sum;
}
```

Memoization

Once we find the number of ways for any number k (0<=k<=X), we can store it in a HashMap with key=k. Alternately, we can use a one-dimensional array and store the number of ways for k at index k in the array.

```
int numWays(int X, int[] cache){
  if(X < 0){ return 0; }
  if(cache[X] == -1){
    if(X == 0){
      cache[X] = 1;
    }else{
```

```
      int sum = 0;
      for(int i=1; i<=6; i++){
        sum += numWays(X-i);
      }
      cache[X] = sum;
    }
  }
  return cache[X];
}
```

Dynamic Programming Solution

The recursion and memoization looks an extrapolation of fibonacci. While calculating a Fibonacci number, we look at the previous two terms, in this case we will look at the previous 6 terms. Number of ways for X=k will be a sum of Number of ways for k-1, k-2, k-3, k-4, k-5, and k-6. So,

```
numWays(10) = numWays(9) + numWays(8) + numWays(7) +
                numWays(6) + numWays(5) + numWays(4)
```

For first six terms, and extra 1 should be added because you can also get that number directly in just one throw.

```
int numWays(int X){
  int[] dp = new int[X+1];

  dp[0] = 0;
  int prev6TermsSum=0;
  // SPECIAL HADLING OF FIRST 6 TERMS
  for(int i=1; i<=6 && i<=X; i++){
    prev6TermsSum += dp[i-1];
    dp[i] = prev6TermsSum + 1;
  }

  for(int i=7; i<=X; i++){
    prev6TermsSum = prev6TermsSum - dp[i-7] + dp[i-1];
    dp[i] = prev6TermsSum;
  }

  return dp[X];
}
```

This code is updating the sum of previous six elements of the dp array inside the loop in constant time using the sliding window approach. Following table shows the result for first 10 values of X.

Like in Fibonacci Series,

Example 6.5 (Sitting arrangement): A college has three streams: Physics (P), Chemistry (C), and Mathematics (M). In the sitting arrangement of the exam, all the students have to sit in a straight line such that no two adjacent students are from the same stream. Given three numbers representing the number of students in three streams, find the number of ways in which we can make all students sit in a single line such that no two adjacent students are from the same streams.

For example, if P=1, C=1, M=0. Then the answer should be 2 because there are two arrangements PC and CP.

Greedy

If we just need to find one possible arrangement (and not count all the arrangements) then we can go with a greedy approach of picking a student from the largest element and make him sit in the first place. After that select an element from the second largest stream and put it in the second place.

At any point pick the student from the largest stream available. Note that we should not consider the stream of previous student.

Recursion

This is a permutation problem, we want to find the permutation of multiple occurrences of three types of elements such that no two adjacent element in the permutation are same.

Another way to look at this is to find all the options possible for a particular position. Let P=2, C=1, M=1.

At the first position, there are three choices, Put a P, or Put a C, or Put a M. If we place a P at the first position, then for the second position there are two options, a C or a M. and so on.. We should either keep track of the previous element or force the next element to exclude the current element. In both situations, we need to have a separate handling for the very first position (because there is no previous element for the first element).

```
// req = 0 FOR P, 1 FOR C, 2 for M
int numWays(int p, int c, int m, int req){
  if (p < 0 || c < 0 || m < 0)
    return 0;

  if(req == 0)
    return (p==1 && c<=0 && m<=0) ?
           1 :
           numWays(p-1,c,m, 1) + numWays(p-1,c,m, 2);

  if(req ==  1)
    return (p<=0 && c==1 && m<=0) ?
           1 :
           numWays(p,c-1,m, 0) + numWays(p,c-1,m, 2);

  if(req ==  2)
    return (p<=0 && c<=0 && m==1) ?
           1 :
           numWays(p,c,m-1, 0) + numWays(p,c,m-1, 1);

  return 0;
}
```

Parameter req tells the above recursive function what to put at the current position. If req=0, put P. If req=1, put C. If req=2, put M. If there is only one student left and that student if from the stream which is required, the answer is 1 (which gets cumulated in recursion).

There are three possibilities for the first position and hence, we should call numWays three times.

```
int numWaysWrapper(int p, int c, int m){
  int x = numWays(p, c, m, 0);
  int y = numWays(p, c, m, 1);
  int z = numWays(p, c, m, 2);
  return x+y+z;
}
```

Such DP problems, where we have to do some pre-processing or post-processing are discussed separately in Chapter-8.

Memoization

The recursion in this case has four variables. You should think of using a four-dimensional array.

```
int[][][][] dp = new int[P][C][M][3];

int numWays(int p, int q, int r, int req)
  if (p < 0 || c < 0 || m < 0)
    return 0;

  if(dp[p][c][m][req] != -1)
  {
    //COMPUTE THE VALUE AND PUT IT IN dp[p][c][m][req]
  }
  return dp[p][c][m][req];
}
```

The logic used will be same as that of recursion. In the DP solution this matrix is populated bottom-up.

Variations of Greedy

Greedy Approach vs Dynamic Programming

Most of the DP problems are related to optimization, ***longest*** common subsequence, ***minimum*** edit distance, ***minimum*** cost path, etc. problems are all trying to optimize something.

There are two approaches to solving an optimization problem that can also be extrapolated to lot of non-optimization problems.

    i. Find all possible solutions to the given problem and then pick the most optimal out of them.
    ii. Just follow your intuition and arrive at a solution that may or may not be optimal.

When a page fault occurs in an LRU cache, the least recently used element is removed and replaced with the new value. It may not give the best-performing cache (most optimal), but it is much faster. Also, it may not be possible to find the best element to be swapped out from the cache because we may not be able to predict the value needed in the future. Most algorithms in operating systems are greedy, be it for CPU scheduling or memory management.

The greedy approach generates a single decision sequence based on localised logic that may not result in the best solution. In some cases, the greedy approach may yield the most optimal solution; however, we need to prove the correctness of that solution to be sure. DP, on the other hand, generates every possible solution and then returns the most optimal of them. Obviously, the DP solution will take more time. In fact, the comparison should be between Greedy and Recursion, with DP simply being a method of optimising recursion.

If that the following graph shows the traffic situation of a city between four points **A**, **B**, **C**, and **D**. The numbers on the edges depict the current traffic situation between two points. For example, it takes 2 minutes to get from point **A** to point **B** and 9 minutes from point **B** to **C**. A person can go from point **A** to point **D** in two ways. The first path (via **B**) costs 11, and the second path (via **C**) costs 6.

$$
\begin{array}{ccc}
 & 9 & \\
\mathbf{B} & \longrightarrow & \mathbf{D} \\
2\uparrow & & \uparrow 1 \\
\mathbf{A} & \longrightarrow & \mathbf{C} \\
 & 5 &
\end{array}
$$

Going towards **B** seems more intuitive to a person standing at point **A** because he may see some traffic heading towards **C**. However, if he follows his intuition (the greedy approach), he will get stuck in a much bigger traffic jam between **B** and **D**. This Greedy approach is not the right way to find the most optimal route in Google Maps. To find the most optimal path, we must find all possible routes from **A** to **D** before selecting the best one, as discussed in Chapter 4.

In the following example, we see a problem that give us the most optimal solution using Greedy approach.

Coin change problem

Example 7.1 (Coin Change Problem): Given an infinite supply of coins of **K** unique denominations, $(V_1, V_2, \ldots, V_K)$ and an integer **N**. Find the minimum number of coins required to give a change of amount **N** using these denominations. For example, if the following array represent denominations of coin/currency notes available:

```
int[] den = {1, 2, 5, 10, 20, 50, 100, 200, 500}
```

then the minimum number of coins required to give a change of N=65 is 3

```
65 = 50+10+5
```

Note that a change of 65 can be given by giving six 10-value notes and one 5-value note, but there will be seven currency notes this way. Like this, there are multiple ways to give a change of 65, but all of them will take more than 3 currency notes. So, giving one 50-value note, one 10-value note and one 5-value note results in minimum number of currency notes.

Greedy Approach

Use the following greedy approach to give a change of N, using the fewest number of currency notes::

"Pick the largest currency denomination available".

Pick the highest currency denomination possible, subtract it from the total, then pick the highest denomination currency note again, and so on.

Pick a 50-value note as the largest currency denomination for 65. Now you want to give a change of 15. The largest currency denomination, for 15, is a 10-value note, so choose 10. Now, for 5, we have a currency denomination of value 5, so choose 5. You can verify that this greedy approach yields the best solution for any value of N. You need to give minimum 3 currency notes to give a change of 65, currency notes being of denominations 50, 10, and 5 each. Following is the code for this logic

- ✓ For 65, the largest currency denomination is of value 50, *pick 50!*
- ✓ Now, you want to give a change of 15, for 15 the largest currency denomination is of value 10, *pick 10*.
- ✓ Now, you should give a change of 5, for that the largest currency is of denomination value 5, *pick 5*.

You can verify that this greedy approach yields the most optimal solution for any value N. You need minimum 3 currency notes to give a change of 65, currency notes being of denominations 50, 10, and 5 each. Following is the code for this logic.

```
int minCoins(int[] den, int N){
  int cnt = 0;
  for(int i=den.length-1; i>=0 ; i--){
```

```
    if(den[i] <= N){
        cnt += N / den[i];
        N = N % den[i];
    }
  }
  return cnt;
}
```

Code: 7.1

This greedy algorithm takes O(k) time, where k is the number of unique currency denominations available (length of the den array). How are you sure that the above solution gives the most optimal value? That is why we must submit proof of correctness for every greedy solution.

Sometimes, you find a Greedy approach and have a strong feeling that it will work for all possible cases because you have tried enough test cases, but you cannot prove the correctness of that algorithm. Fortunately, you can submit a code to the interviewer and delegate the burden of proving it wrong to the interviewer. The interviewer must provide a counter-example or test case for which our code fails. However, in academia, you are almost always required to prove the correctness of our greedy approach.

Proof of correctness

Let C50, C20, C10, C5, C2, and C1 respectively, be the number of fifties, twenties, tens, fives, twos, and ones in the change generated by the greedy algorithm, and let Co50, Co20, Co10, Co5, Co2, and Co1, respectively, be the number of fifties, twenties, tens, fives, twos, and ones in the change generated by the optimal algorithm.

Make the following observations:

The sum provided by a lower denomination is always less than the value of the next higher denomination. i.e the change given in value-1 notes should be less than value-2 because if it is equal to value-2, you will give a value-2 note instead. Similarly, the sum provided by value-2 notes should be less than value-3. Therefore,

C20 < 3, C10 < 2, C5 < 2, C2 < 3 and C1 < 2

You can establish the above rule for the most optimal solution also. i.e

Co20 < 3, Co10 < 2, Co5 < 2, Co2 < 3 and Co1 < 2

If Co20 >=3, you can replace three twenties with a fifty and a ten and provide the change using one less currency note.

Similarly, for the other denominations. Therefore, the total change given in lower denominations is less than the value of the next higher denomination.

If C50 != Co50, either the greedy or the optimal solution must provide 50 or more in lower denominations. This violates the above observations. Therefore, C50 = Co50. Similarly, it can be proved for all other denominations. Hence greedy solution is same as the most optimal solution.

Greedy Approach does not always work.

Will the greedy solution of Code 7.1 also work if the government introduces a new currency note worth value-12.

```
int[] den = {1, 2, 5, 10, 12, 20, 50, 100, 200, 500}
```

Let us try. Apply the same greedy approach,

"Pick the largest currency denomination available".

Using the above denominations, the greedy approach will result in four currency notes for a change of N=65, as shown below:

- ✓ For 65, the largest currency note is value-50. *Pick 50!*
- ✓ Now, you want to give 15, for 15, the largest currency note is value-12 (and not 10). *Pick 12!*
- ✓ Now, you want to give 3 more, for which you should give two currency notes of 2 and 1 each.

Hence, four currency notes in total. We already know that a change of 65 can be given using 3 currency notes. Why is the greedy solution failing for this denomination?

If the greedy solution does not work, how can we solve it? The answer is simple; consider all possible ways to give a change of 65 and choose the most optimal one. It will take more time but will ensure an optimal result. Considering all possible ways is, 'Dynamic Programming' and DP starts with Recursion.

Recursive Solution

The minimum number of coins for a value **N** can be computed using below Include-Exclude logic. At each currency denomination, there are two options,

    i.   **Include** it in the change that you are providing.
    ii.   **Do not include** it in the change that you are providing.

When you include the current currency in the change (first option), you may want to include same currency again; however, when you exclude the current currency (second option), then it is excluded. If the current currency is at index i in the den array, and the problem statement is *"Find the min number of currency notes required to give a change of* N *starting from index-i in the* den *array"*. The above options translate to the below logic for index-i:

    i.   **Include** den[i] in the change. Now, *"Find the min number of currency notes required to give a change of* N-den[i] *starting from index-i in the* den *array"*. We remain at index-i because this denomination may get included again (e.x., to give a change of 45, value-20 is included twice).
    ii.   **Do not include** den[i] in the change. Now, *"Find the min number of currency notes required to give a change of* N *starting from index-*(i+1) *in the* den *array*. The denomination at index-i will not be part of the change.

The final answer is the minimum of above two options. Notice the recursion in above options. Also note that including the current currency is not always an option. You can include the current currency only if it is not larger than the change you want to give. Following is the recursive code for above logic (It assumes that the den array is sorted)

```
int minCoins(int[] den, int N, int i){
  // TERMINATING CONDITIONS
  if(N == 0)
    return 0;
```

```
if(i>=den.length || den[i] > N)
  return -1; // IMPOSSIBLE TO GIVE THE CHANGE

int x = minCoins(den, N-den[i], i);  //INCLUDE den[i]
int y = minCoins(den, N, i+1);       // EXLUDE den[i]

if(x == -1 && y == -1){ return -1; } // NO OPTION
if(x == -1){ return y; }             // ONLY 1 OPTION
if(y == -1){ return x+1; }           // ONLY 1 OPTION

return getMin(x+1, y);
}
```

Code: 7.2

An extra 1 is added in the include option because one currency note is included in the change. This solution takes exponential time in the worst case. If you draw the recursion tree (function call tree), you will observe that subproblems are overlapping. That makes it a good candidate for Dynamic Programming.

We can also use memoization to avoid having to solve the same subproblem multiple times. An array of size (N+1) can be used as a cache and the minCoins value of N=x can be stored at index x in the array. When the function is called again for N=x, a lookup happens in the cache array and this value is returned without recomputing it again.

Following non-recursive DP solution populates this array bottom-up.

Dynamic Programming Solution

The DP solution uses a two-dimensional array. There are two reasons for using a two-dimensional array: one, that is what we used as a cache in memoization, and two, there are two variables (index of the den array and N). If N=11, values along one dimension range from 0 to 11. The other dimension contains den array index representing the current denomination. Consider the following diagram. The highlighted cell in the diagram will store the minimum currency notes required to give a change of 6 when the current index of den array is 1 (i.e den[1] = 2).

With the current currency denomination as 2 (at index 1 in the den array), there are following two options.

154

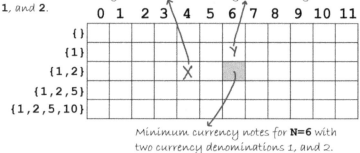

Minimum currency notes required for N=4 with two currency denominations 1, and 2.

Minimum currency notes for **N=6** with only one currency denominations **1**.

Minimum currency notes for **N=6** with two currency denominations 1, and 2.

i. Include 2 in the change. Now, *"Find the min number of currency notes required to give a change of* 4 *with index-1 as last element in the* den *array"*. This value is in the cell marked as **X** in the diagram.

ii. Do not include 2 in the change. Now, *"Find the min number of currency notes required to give a change of* 6 *with index-0 as last element in the* den *array"*. This value is in the cell marked as **Y** in the diagram.

Before applying the above logic, use the terminating conditions of recursion to initialise the top row and first column.

```
int minCoins(int[] den, int N){
  int k = den.length+1;
  int[][] res = new int[k][N+1];

  // INITIALIZATION
  for(int i=0; i<k; i++) // IF N=0
    res[i][0] = 0;
  for(int i=1; i<N+1; i++)
    res[0][i] = -1; // IF den ARRAY IS EMPTY AND N>0

  for(int i=1; i<k; i++){
    for(int j=1; j<N+1; j++){
      // CURRENT DEN = den[i-1]. N=j
      if(j<den[i-1]) // ONLY OPTION = EXCLUDE
        res[i][j] = res[i-1][j];
      else{
        int x = res[i][j-den[i-1]]; // INCLUDE
        int y = res[i-1][j]; // EXCLUDE

        if(x==-1 && y == -1){res[i][j] = -1; }
        else if(y == -1){ res[i][j] = x+1; }
        else if(x == -1){ res[i][j] = y; }
```

```
        else { res[i][j] = getMin(x+1, y); }
    }
  }
}
return res[k-1][N];
}
```

Code: 7.3

In the above solution, we are also considering the possibility when it is impossible to provide the change of a value.

Question 7.1: In the above problem, there was an infinite supply of coins/notes of each currency denomination. What if there are a limited number of currency notes? Change the above solution for a case when you are also given the number of available currency notes for every denomination.

Hint: The inclusion of a particular currency is also dependent on the availability of notes of that denomination.

Question 7.2: Given a set of coins and an amount, write an algorithm to find out how many ways we can make the change of the amount using the coins given.

Knapsack problem

Example 7.2: A thief carries a knapsack (bag) with a maximum capacity of W kg. He breaks into a shop that has N items. Determine the maximum value that the thief can carry given the weight of each item (present in the shop) and the total value of that item. For example, let capacity of the knapsack be W=60kg and weight and price of each item available in the shop is as given in the following table (along with the name of item),

	Wheat	Rice	Pulses	Sugar
Weight (kg)	15	30	20	10
Value ($)	105	180	180	100

The total amount of wheat available in the shop is 30kg, but the thief can take a portion of that, say 10kg out of the total 30kg if he wants. Because the thief can pick a fraction of the product, this variation of the knapsack problem is called **Fractional Knapsack**. Later, we will see another variation, where it wont be possible to pick a portion of the item, and the thief has to either pick, or leave the entire item. But first, let us look at the Greedy solution of Fractional Knapsack.

Greedy Solution

Find the Value/Weight ratio for each item and select the items in decreasing order of this ratio. The ratio is listed below each column in the following table.

	Wheat	Rice	Pulses	Sugar
Weight (kg)	15	30	20	10
Value ($)	105	180	180	100
$/kg →	7	6	9	10

The thief should first pick the maximum quantity of the most valuable item in terms of value/weight. The capacity of his knapsack is 60kg, so the thief can pick up the entire 10kg of Sugar. After picking 10kg of Sugar, the remaining capacity of the bag is 50kg. The next item to be picked is pulses and wheat, in this order. After picking all three of them the total value in the bag is 100+105+180 = 385$, and the weight of the bag is 10+20+15 = 45kg. The remaining capacity of the bag is 15 kg. He can pick 15kg of Rice, making the total value in the bag 385+90 =475$. It can be proved that this is the maximum value the thief can steal from the shops.

This is a greedy approach in which we followed our intuition rather than considering all possible combinations of picking the items.

Binary Knapsack

Consider what would happen if the same thief entered an electronics store instead of a grocery shop. He cannot partially pick up the items inside an electronic store. For example, consider the following table showing the weight and values of items in an electronic store,

	A.C	Fridge	T.V	Battery
Weight (kg)	15	30	20	10
Value ($)	105	180	180	100

The thief cannot pick half of the Fridge. Every item has a binary choice; either it is completely picked, or not picked at all. The previous greedy approach will not give the most optimal value for this Binary Knapsack problem. If he picks the items using the previous logic, then it will pick only Battery, T.V, and A.C with a total value of 385$ and 15kg of the bag is still empty. A better solution is to pick Fridge, T.V, and Battery with a total value of 460$.

If greedy approach does not work, we must find all possible ways of picking the items and pick the most optimal solution from among them.

Recursive Solution

This problem's brute force recursive logic is very similar to the coin change problem. There are two choices for each item in the shop,

   i.   Add the item to the bag, or
  ii. Do not add the item to the bag.

This represents an exponential increase in options, and such problems are solved through recursion as illustrated in Figure 7.1

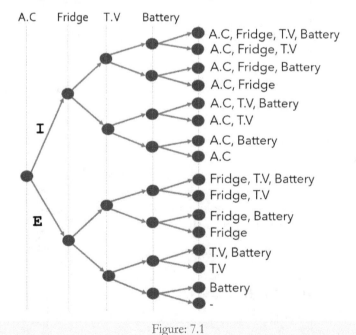

Figure: 7.1

There are two options for each item: include it in the bag or exclude it. The upper arrow in the diagram represents the Include path, while the lower arrow represents the Exclude path. The result of each recursive function call is shown on the right side. For example, if you keep including everything, then at the end you will have A.C, Fridge, T.V, and Battery. This may or may not be a valid option depending on the capacity of the bag. We should discard the options where the total weight of picked items is greater than the total capacity of the bag. The most optimal out of all the valid options is the final answer.

The original problem statement is to *"Find the maximum value when capacity of the bag is* W *and we are at index-0* (In the list of items)."

i. If 0th item is included in the bag, the problem reduces to, *"Find the maximum value when capacity of the bag is* W-weight[0] *and we are at index-1"*. Add value[0] to the result of this subproblem.

ii. If 0th item is not included in the bag, the problem reduces to, *"Find the maximum value when capacity of the bag is* W *and we are at index-1."*

Our final answer is the larger of above two options. Following is the code for above logic.

```
int binKS(int[] wght, int[] val, int W, int i){

    // IF NO ITEM LEFT OR BAG FULL
    if(i == wght.length || W == 0)
        return 0;

    // IF WEIGHT OF CURRENT ITEM > CAPACITY. EXCLUDE.
    if(wght[i] > W)
        return binKS(wght, val, W, i+1);

    // INCLUDE
    int x = val[i] + binKS(wght, val, W-wght[i], i+1);

    // EXCLUDE
    int y = binKS(wght, val, W, i+1);

    return getMax(x, y);
}
```

Code: 7.4

Code 7.4 takes exponential time, $O(2^n)$, and has overlapping subproblems.

Memoization

Like in the previous problem, the cache for this memoization is a two dimensional array of order `(W+1) * (N+1)`, where `W` is capacity of the bag and `N` is the number of items in the bag. `cache[i][j]` store the maximum value the thief can get if capacity of bag = `i` and there are only first `j` items in the store.

Dynamic Programming Solution

The DP solution to this problem will populate the matrix bottom-up, from the first cell to the last. The logic for populating the matrix is very similar to the logic used in Example 7.1's DP solution. First the top row and leftmost column are populated using the logic of recursion's terminating conditions.

```
int knapSack(int[] weight, int[] val, int W){
  int N = val.length;
  int[][] res = new int[N+1][W+1];

  // INITIALIZING TOP ROW (NO ITEM)
  for(int i=0; i<W+1; i++)
    res[0][i] = 0;

  // INITIALIZING FIRST COL (CAPACITY OF BAG = 0)
  for(int i=0; i<N+1; i++)
    res[i][0] = 0;

  for (int i=1; i<N+1; i++){
    for (int cp=1; cp<W+1; cp++){
      if (weight[i-1] > cp)
        res[i][cp] = res[i-1][cp];
      else{
        int x = val[i-1] + res[i-1][cp-weight[i-1]];
        int y = res[i-1][cp];
        res[i][cp] = getMax(x, y);
      }
    }
  }
  return res[N][W];
}
```

Code: 7.5

Code 7.5 takes polynomial time, `O(N.W)`. Let capacity of the bag be `W=5` and there are four items with the following weight and values,

weight	2	3	4	5
Val	3	4	5	6

Then the `res` table of Code 7.5 is populated as following and the final answer is 7.

Items

Weight →		0	1	2	3	4	5
	0	0	0	0	0	0	0
	1	0	0	3	3	3	3
	2	0	0	3	4	4	7
	3	0	0	3	4	5	7
	4	0	0	3	4	5	7

Question 7.3: Modify the above solution to also print the items that are picked in the final solution.

Question 7.4: In the example of binary knapsack, there was only one piece of each item in the store (one Fridge, one A.C, etc). What if there are multiple pieces of each item in the store? For example, in the following example, there are 5 A.C, 3 Fridge, 7 T.V and 2 Batteries in the store.

	A.C	Fridge	T.V	Battery
Weight (kg)	15	30	20	10
Value ($)	105	180	180	100
Quantity	5	3	7	2

Conclusion

Is Dynamic Programming better than the Greedy Approach? Is a leather jacket better than a cotton t-shirt? Depends on the weather!

Both DP and Greedy are typically used to solve optimization problems. Every problem has specific properties that "naturally force" you to choose either DP or greedy, but not both.

However, if you come across a problem that can be solved using both DP and greedy, choose greedy. Because greedy traverses the problem space much more quickly and is quite simple to implement. On the other hand, DP is exhaustive and must take into account all possible subproblems.

Miscellaneous

Some DP problems do not fit into any of the templates discussed in previous chapters in this section because they do not follow any fixed pattern. I am trying to cover such questions in this chapter. I do not claim that it is an exhaustive list of all the questions. The list of DP questions is constantly growing, with new DP questions added frequently.

Recursion has a wrapper.

In some cases, some work must be completed prior to the start of the core logic (recursion) or after the completion of core logic of recursion. This work can be completed within a wrapper function. The entire solution now consists of three parts rather than one, which are executed in a sequence, and a different approach may be required.

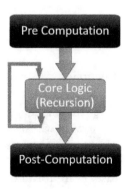

Example 8.1: (Goldmine problem) Given a gold mine represented by a two-dimensional array of

N*M dimensions. In this mine, each field contains a positive integer representing the amount of gold in that cell. The miner is standing on the left side of the matrix (before the first column). From any cell, he can only move to the right cell, right-up cell, or right-down cell, as shown below.

		i-1, j-1
i,j →	i, j-1	
		i+1, j-1

Determine the maximum amount of gold he can collect on the way. For example, if the following matrix represents a goldmine,

MINER

2	1	1	6	1
5	2	4	3	2
3	1	7	2	5
1	8	6	1	2
2	3	2	2	3

The Miner can start digging from any cell in the first column. But, when he selects a cell, he can only move to a connected cell in the next column which is either in the same row, diagonally-up, or diagonally-down. There are multiple options, each resulting in a fixed amount of gold. For example, the following two paths, will yield 18kg and 21kg gold, respectively. Also note that the path that leads to the maximum gold may not begin with the largest element of the first column.

2	1	1	6	1
5	2	4	3	2
3	1	7	2	5
1	8	6	1	2
2	3	2	2	3

Amt.= 5+1+4+3+5 = 18

Amt.= 2+8+6+2+3 = 21

Recursion

Once the miner is in a cell, he has three options (unless he is in the first or last row, in which case he only has two). But for the very first step, there are M options (equal to the number of rows). This means that the first step of miner needs to be handled separately. Also, the natural recursion in this case is in forward direction starting from the first column. Following function list the recursion when the miner is in cell (i,j).

```
int maxGold(int[][] gold, int i, int j){
    int m = a.length;
    int n = gold[0].length;

    // OUTSIDE THE MATRIX
    if(i<0 || i>=m || j>=n){
        return 0;
    }
    // IN THE LAST COLUMN
    if(j == n-1){
        return gold[i][j];
    }

    int x = maxGold(gold, i-1, j+1);
    int y = maxGold(gold, i, j+1);
    int z = maxGold(gold, i+1, j+1);

    return gold[i][j] + getMax(x, y, z);
}
```

Code: 8.1

If we know the starting cell, we can use this recursion to find the maximum gold that can be collected if the miner starts from that cell and also the path to collect that gold. For instance, the following function call:

```
maxGold(gold, 2, 0));
```

will return the maximum gold that can be collected if he starts from cell $(2, 0)$. So, we should call the above recursion for all possible starting cells.

```
int getMaxGold(int[][] gold){
    int maxVal = 0;
    for (int i = 0; i < gold.length; i++) {
        int val = maxGold(gold, i, 0);
        maxVal = Math.max(val, maxVal);
    }
    return maxVal;
}
```

Above function will be called from outside and it acts as a wrapper over the function in Code 8.1 that contains the main logic.

Memoization

The natural choice of cache in this question is a two-dimensional array where cache[i][j] stores the maximum amount of gold that can be collected from cell (i, j). If the value is already computed, then we will just do a lookup into the cache, otherwise we should compute the value and store it in that cell.

Dynamic Programming

Take a two-dimensional array and use the logic of recursion in Code 8.1 to populate the matrix starting from the last column.

First use the terminating condition of recursion to initialize the last column of the array.

				1
				2
				5
				2
				3

```
for(int i=0; i<m; i++)
    a[i][n-1] = gold[i][n-1];
```

Now populate the matrix column-wise starting from the 2nd last column using the logic of recursion.

```
for(int c=n-2; c>=0; c--){
    int max = a[i][j];
    if(i > 0 && a[i-1][j] > max)
        max = a[i-1][j];
    if(i < m-1 && a[i+1][j] > max)
        max = a[i+1][j];

    a[i][j] = gold[i][j] + max;
}
```

19	13	9	8	1
22	17	12	8	2
26	16	15	7	5
24	23	13	6	2
25	16	8	5	3

Once the matrix is populated as shown above, the final answer is the maximum value in the first column, i.e 26. The DP solution takes $O(m*n)$ time.

We can get the path of maximum gold by tracing the path starting from maximum cell.

19	13	9	8	1
22	17	12	8	2
26	16	15	7	5
24	23	13	6	2
25	16	8	5	3

If something needs to be done to allow recursion to begin while developing a recursive solution, do it in the wrapper function. For instance, the recursion of Graph's DFS (Depth First Search) algorithm requires a visited

HashSet as a parameter. Expecting the calling function to create a HashSet and pass it to the DFS makes no sense. It's best to do it in a wrapper function.

Using non-recursive concepts to solve.

When an interviewer asks a question, he does not specify whether the question is from DP, Greedy, or Backtracking, for example. He will simply present you with a problem that must be solved. You have to figure out the data structure and algorithm that will be used to solve the given problem. In mathematics, two people can solve the same problem using two completely different concepts and formulae and still get the same answer.

There are some DP problems where recursion is not the first (or most intuitive) solution. Let us look at an example.

Example 8.2 (Dropping Eggs): You have two identical eggs and access to a 100-floor building. You don't know how strong the eggs are. Eggs can be extremely strong (not breaking if dropped from the 100th floor), or extremely fragile (breaking if dropped from the first floor), or somewhere in between. Determine the minimum number of drops needed to find the highest floor from which an egg can be dropped without breaking. You may break both eggs in the process.

Even though this is a DP problem and we are trying to optimize the number of drops, the DP (or recursive) solution may not be the first one to strike the mind. This is essentially a search problem and we are searching for the height floor that does not break the egg. We usually use linear search, binary search, or a variation of these for searching. Sometimes a HashMap/HashSet type of data structure is also used to improve search, but this question does not have such a scenario.

Linear Search Solution:

- Start from the first floor, and keep moving one floor up at a time. From each floor drop the egg and see if it breaks.
- If the egg breaks at the k'th floor, then Answer is k-1.
- If the egg does not break at all then the answer is 100.

Note that this is the only way to find the answer if there is only one egg. Number of Drops in the worst case = 100. Can we use Binary search?

Binary Search Solution:

In this solution, use Binary Search logic with the first egg. The Binary Search logic uses the Divide & Conquer approach and divides the current interval in 2 equal halves. Following is the algorithm

```
Low = 0
While(Low < 100)
  Mid = (Low + 100)/2
  Drop the first egg from Mid floor
    IF First egg breaks
      FOR n = Low TO Mid-1 (both included)
        Drop Second Egg from nth floor
        IF it breaks
          Answer is (n-1)
      IF Second Egg does not break at all
        Answer is Mid-1
    ELSE              // First egg does not break.
      L = Mid+1
Answer is 100    // IF EGG DOES NOT BREAK ATT ALL
```

Please note that, after the first egg breaks, the second egg should be tried linearly. In the base case the first egg will not break till the very last attempt and total number of drops will be $\lg(n)$. However, in the worst case, the number of drops are 50. This happens when the first egg breaks in the very first drop (from the 50th floor) and the second egg does not break in 49 attempts (or break in the 49th attempt). The first egg is dropped 1 time and second one 49 times, making the total number of drops equal to 50.

Fixed Interval Solution:

The issue with the Binary Search solution is that it applies the Binary Search logic to the first egg but not the second. Once the first egg has broken, the second egg must scan the current interval linearly. The earlier the first egg breaks, The longer the interval for the second egg.

The next thought which may come is what if we fix the interval size ?

Assume the first egg is dropped after a fixed interval of, say, ten floors. Drop the first egg from the 10th, 20th, 30th, and so on up to the 100th floor. If the first egg breaks from, say, the 70th floor, we must try the second egg from the 61st to the 69th floor in the worst-case scenario.

```
int k=10                      // INTERVAL SIZE = 10
WHILE (k <=100)
  Drop First egg from kth floor
  IF First Egg breaks
    FOR n = k-9 TO k-1 (both included)
      Drop Second Egg from nth floor
      IF it breaks
        Answer is (n-1)
  IF Second Egg does not break at all
    Answer is k-1
  ELSE                 // First Egg does not break
    k = k+10
Answer is 100   // IF EGG DOES NOT BREAK ATT ALL
```

In the worst case, the number of drops is 19, when the first egg breaks from the 100th floor and the second egg breaks from the 99th floor or does not break at all.

You may argue that what will happen if we reduce the interval size from 10 to, say, 5?

Well in that case, the number of drops in the worst case will be 24. Because in the worst case, the first egg needs to be dropped 20 times (because there are 20 intervals) and the second egg should be dropped 4 times (because the size of each interval is 5).

What if we increase the interval to say, 20?

Again the total number of drops in the worst case will be 24 because the first egg needs to be dropped 5 times (because there are 5 intervals) and the second egg should be dropped 19 times (because size of each interval is 20).

You may confirm that the best result will come when interval size if 10 and the minimum number of drops in the worst case for this logic is 19..

We have come a long way, but can we do better than 19? In this logic each interval is of same size, what if we have intervals of different size?

The number of drops in the baset case using this logic is 2. The best case comes when the first egg breaks from the 10th floor and the second egg breaks from the 1st floor itself. So total number of drops is 2.

Variable Interval Solution:

In the previos solution, what if the First egg behaves like the best case (i.e breaks in the first drop itself) and second egg behaves like the worst case (i.e takes the maximum number of drops). The total number of drops will be 1+9 = 10. Let us look at the worst case of second egg for different possibilities of the first egg.

Possibility	1st egg	2nd egg Worst case	Total # of drops
If first egg breaks from 10th floor	1	9	10
If first egg breaks from 20th floor	2	9	11
If first egg breaks from 30th floor	3	9	12
If first egg breaks from 40th floor	4	9	13
If first egg breaks from 50th floor	5	9	14
If first egg breaks from 60th floor	6	9	15
If first egg breaks from 70th floor	7	9	16
If first egg breaks from 80th floor	8	9	17
If first egg breaks from 90th floor	9	9	18
If first egg breaks from 100th floor	10	9	19

The above table shows the total number of drops for different possibilities of the first egg, assuming that the second egg always gives the worst case result. Because the size of each interval is 10, the second egg must be dropped 9 times for each interval in the worst case. The overall worst case is 19 when both the eggs takes worst case time.

What happens if we reduce the size of the last interval by one and increase the size of the first interval by one? Now, the number of drops for the first interval will be 11 (because the size of this interval is increased), and the worst case for the last interval will be 18 (because the size of this interval is decreased). The overall worst case is now reduced by one and we have increased the number of drops in the best case of first egg by one. Similarly, we can further reduce the interval size of last few rows and distribute then to the first few rows, this will increase the number of drops in the first few rows reducing the number of drops in the later rows untill the total number of drops in all the rows become same, say x.

If x is the number of drops required to find the correct floor number.

If the first egg breaks after one drop, we can have x-1 drops left. So, the first interval will be of length x.

Drop the first egg from floor-x. If it breaks, the second egg needs to be dropped x-1 times in the worst case. Total number of drops = x.

If the first egg does not break in its First Drop (from height x). Then drop it after x-1 floors, i.e keep the size of second interval as x-1.

Drop the first egg from floor (x+ (x-1)). If it breaks, the second egg needs to be dropped x-2 times in the worst case. Total number of drops = x.

Every time the first egg does not break, reduce the interval size by 1 so that the total number of drops in each case is x.

From the above solution, it is clear that the optimal solution will require 0 linear trials in the last step. Hence, the corresponding mathematical equation for 100 floors is:

X + (X-1) + (X-2) + ... + (1) >= 100

Solving the equation, we get
X = 14.

The size of the first interval is 14 and so is the minimum number of drops.

i.e drop the first egg from following floors until it breaks: 14, 27, 39, 50, 60, 69, 77, 84, 90, 95, 99, 100. If at any point it breaks, start the 2'nd egg linearly from (previous floor + 1).

Dynamic Programming Solution

In the above solution, we did not discuss DP at all. It appears as if it is not a DP problem. But we can think of a recursion that has overlapping subproblems.

When an egg is dropped from floor x, one of two things can happen: it either breaks or it does not.

- ✓ If the egg breaks from floor-x, we only need to look for floors less than x, with the second egg (or remaining eggs, in case we have more than one eggs), reducing the problem to x-1 floors and 1 egg.
- ✓ If the egg does not break after dropping from floor-x, we only need to check for floors greater than x with the first egg itself (because it is not yet broken), reducing the problem to '100-x' floors and 2 eggs.

The final answer will be the minimum of above two. If there are N floors and k eggs, then we have to try the above two options for each floor. Number of drops in the worst case will be

```
minDrops(N, k) = 1 + min{ max( minDrops(x-1, k-1),
                              minDrops(N-x, k),…
                    FOR EACH x IN 1 TO N) }
```

You can add the terminating conditions in the above recursion. There are two variables, hence a two-dimensional array should be used in the bottom-up DP solution.

```
int minDrops(int n, int k){
  int[][] dp = new int[k + 1][n + 1];
  int res;

  // IF 0 or 1 FLOOR THAN NO DROPS
  for(int i=1; i<=k; i++) {
    dp[i][1] = 1;
    dp[i][0] = 0;
  }

  for(int j=1; j<=n; j++) // IF ONLY 1 EGG
    dp[1][j] = j;

  for(int i=2; i<=k; i++) {
    for(int j=2; j<=n; j++) {
      dp[i][j] = Integer.MAX_VALUE;
      for(int x=1; x<=j; x++) {
        int val = 1+getMax(dp[i-1][x-1], dp[i][j-x]);
        if(val < dp[i][j])
          dp[i][j] = val;
      }
    }
  }
  return dp[k][n];
}
```

What I'm trying to say with this example is that you might come across a completely different approach to solving a DP problem than the ones you have read or studied in academics.

There is a special case.

There are some DP problems where special cases must be hardcoded. Finding such scenarios can be difficult, so try to remember all such questions you encounter. Consider one such example.

Example 8.3 (Filling a rectangle with fewest squares): Given a rectangle of size n*m (1<=m,n<=13). Find the minimum number of squares that can cover the complete rectangle. Sides of all the square should be integer. Following are some examples,

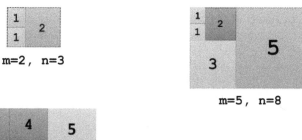

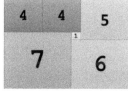

3 squares are sufficient to cover a rectangle of dimension 2*3. We need minimum 5 squares to cover a rectangle of size 5*8 and minimum 6 squares to cover a 11*13 rectangle.

Recursive Solution

The first thought that comes to the mind is to consider all the options for a square starting from one corner of the rectangle and generate the subproblems. Length of the square at a of the rectangle can range from 1 to min(m,n). If we put a square at the bottom-left corner of the rectangle, then rest of the rectangle can be divided into two rectangles (which can be solved recursively.

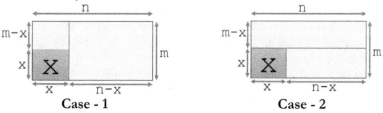

In the first case, we are left with two rectangles of dimensions (m-x)*x and (n-x)*m. In the second case we are left with two rectangles of dimension

(m-x)*n and (n-x)*x. Values of x will range from 1 to min(m,n). Now these two cases can be solved seperately and the result will be minimum of the two.

But wait! What about the third example (m=11, n=13). Well, this is the special case and can be hardcoded.

The challenge in this problem is to figure out that the third case is the only exception and can be handled separately. You may come up with this by

```
int numWays(int m, int n){
  if(m == 0 || n == 0){ return 0; }
  if(m == 1){ return n; }
  if(n == 1){ return m; }
  if(m == n){ return 1; }
  if((m==11 && n==13)||(m==13 && n==1)){ return 6; }

  int minVal = Integer.MAX_VALUE;
  for(int x=1; x <= getMin(m, n); x++){
    int a = numWays(m-x, x) + numWays(m, n-x) + 1;
    int b = numWays(m-x, n) + numWays(x, n-x) + 1;
    minVal = getMin(a, b, minVal);
  }
  return minVal;
}
```

If you know the special case, it is not difficult to come up with this recursion. Once we have the above recursion, we know what to do next. This recursion has overlapping subproblems that can be fixed using memoization or DP. The cache of memoization will be a two-dimensional array because there are two variables. cache[i][j] will store the minimum number of squares required to cover a rectangle of size i*j.

Dynamic Programming

The DP solution will use a two dimensional array of size (m+1) * (n+1) and will populate the array bottom-up using the logic of recursion. For some values of parameters, we do not even need to populate the matrix as shown in the following Code

```
int tilingRectangle(int n, int m) {
  // DIRECT HANDLING OF SOME VALUES
  if(m == 0 || n == 0){ return 0; }
  if(m == 1){ return n; }
  if(n == 1){ return m; }
  if((m==11 && n==13) || (n==11 && m==13))
```

```
      return 6;

  // a[i][j] STORES MIN SQUARES FOR i*j RECTANGLE
  int[][] a = new int[m+1][n+1];
  for(int i=0; i<=m; i++){ a[i][0] = 0; }
  for(int i=0; i<=n; i++){ a[0][i] = 0; }

  for(int i=1; i<=m; i++){
    for(int j=1; j<=n; j++){
      if(i == j)
          a[i][j] = 1;
      else{
          int val1 = Integer.MAX_VALUE;
          int val2 = Integer.MAX_VALUE;
          int min = Integer.MAX_VALUE;
          for(int x=1; x<=Math.min(i,j); x++){
            val1 = a[i][j-x] + a[i-x][x];
            val2 = a[i-x][j] + a[x][j-x];
            min = Math.min(val1, Math.min(val2, min));
          }
          a[i][j] = min+1;
      }
    }
  }
  return a[m][n];
}
```

Brute-Force is not direct Recursion.

There are some DP problems where brute-force logic is not intuitively recursive. However, because there are many overlapping subproblems, you can visualise the application of memoization and then tabulation or DP. Consider the following example,

Example 8.4 (Minimum Cost of Pyramid): A subarray is called a pyramid if the first element of the subarray is 1, and then elements continuously increase by one until they reach some maximum value x (height of the pyramid), and after that values decrease by one until they reach 1 again. For example, $\{1, 2, 3, 4, 3, 2, 1\}$ is a pyramid. You may have 0's on the left and right side of the pyramid. For example, all the following arrays are pyramids,
$\{1, 2, 1, 0, 0, 0\}$, $\{0, 0, 1, 2, 1\}$, $\{0, 0, 1, 2, 1, 0, 0\}$

Given an array of N non-negative integers. You cannot move any element from its current position, but the value of an element can be reduced by paying a fee of 1 per unit of reduction (the cost of changing 5 to 3 is 2). Finding the minimum cost of converting the array to pyramid.

For example, the minimum cost of changing array {1,2,3,4,2,1} to pyramid is 4. The pyramid will be {1,2,3,2,1,0} which we can get by subtracting 2 from 4, and 1 each from 2 and 1.

Redefining the problem statement

It can be proved that the pyramid with the lowest construction cost is the one with the highest possible height. Furthermore, two pyramids of the equal height will cost the same amount to build from scratch (when array has all zeros).

If the total cost of reducing all the elements to zero is x. and the total cost of razing a pyramid of height h is y, then the cost of creating a pyramid of height h from the given array is $(x-y)$.

Now, we can find the pyramid of maximum height that can be formed instead of finding the minimum cost of forming the pyramid. Once the maximum-height pyramid is formed and the starting point (or peak-point) of the pyramid is known, we can calculate the cost required for each element.

> *One of the important things is problem-solving is to redefine the problem is our own words and approach it from a completely different angle than the way it was originally perceived.*

Brute-Force Solution

For each position in the array, find the maximum height of pyramid that can be formed with that point at the centre.

To find the maximum height of the pyramid centred at int k, first initialize it to the value at index k.

```
maxHeight = arr[k]
```

Now, scan the array toward left from index-k and see if this max height needs to be reduced. For example, if arr[k-1] is less than arr[k]-1, then set the maxHeight to arr[k-1]+1. Similarly, scan on the right side of index k.

```java
// FIND MAX HEIGHT IF k IS THE CENTRE OF PYRAMID
public static int getMaxHeight(int[] a, int k){
  int maxH = a[k];

  for(int i=k-1; i>=0 ; i--){
    int d = k-i;   // DISTANCE FROM CENTRE OF PYRAMID
    if(a[i] < maxH-d){
      maxH = a[i]+d;
    }
  }

  for(int i=k+1; i<a.length ; i++){
    int d = i-k;   // DISTANCE FROM CENTRE OF PYRAMID
    if(a[i] < maxH-d){
      maxH = a[i]+d;
    }
  }
  return maxH;
}
```

Find the maximum height pyramid for each index and return the maximum out of all of them. Once we find the maximum height and the centre point of pyramid, we can easily find the cost of constructing such a pyramid in linear time.

The overall time taken by this algorithm will be $O(N^2)$.

> *Not every DP problem has an exponential-time Brute-force solution. Similarly, Not Every DP problem has a recursive Brute-Force solution.*

Even though there is no recursion in this solution, there are overlapping subproblems. Because there is no recursion, we must determine whether the solution exhibits optimal substructure. To find the maximum height at a point we must know the maximum height of points on the left and on the right. Hence, optimal substructure.

Dynamic Programming Solution

In the Brute-Force, we are scanning on both sides of an index, left and right. In DP, we will build the two arrays separately (or you may use a two-dimensional array). Let us call these arrays left and right `left[k]` will hold the maximum height of a pyramid centred at k by only looking on the left side of k, assuming the right side will never reduce it.

`right[k]` will hold the maximum height of a pyramid centred at k by only looking on the right side of k, assuming the left side will never reduce it.

The left array should be populated using the following logic
`maxHeight(k) = Min(a[k], k+1, maxHeight(k-1)+1)`

The maximum height cannot exceed the value at a[k] because we cannot increase any value. The maximum height cannot be more than k+1 which is the value that we get if we start the pyramid at index-0 itself, the starting point of pyramid cannot be before 0. Similarly, the maximum height of a pyramid centred at index-k can only exceed the maximum height pyramid centred at k-1 by 1 and not more.

Calculate similar values for each index from right to left and store those values in the `right` array. The final value for each position will be the minimum of values for that position in the `left` and `right` array.

```
static int minCost(int[] a){
    int n = a.length;
    int[] left = new int[n];
    int[] right = new int[n];

    // POPULATE left ARRAY
    left[0] = getMin(a[0],1); //MIN HEIGHT CENTRED AT 0
    for(int i=1; i<n; i++){
        left[i] = getMin(a[i], i+1, left[i-1]+1);
    }

    // POPULATE right ARRAY
    right[n-1]=getMin(a[n-1],1);
    for(int i=n-2; i>=0; i--){
        right[i] = getMin(a[i], n-i, right[i+1]+1);
    }

    // FIND MAX HEIGHT OF PYRAMING
    int maxIdx = 0;
    int maxHeight = getMin(left[0], right[0]);
    for(int i=1; i<n; i++){
        if(maxHeight < getMin(left[i], right[i])){
            maxIdx = i;
            maxHeight = getMin(left[i], right[i]);
        }
```

```
}

// CALCULATING COST
int cost = a[maxIdx]-maxHeight;

// COST ON LEFT SIDE
int h = maxHeight-1;
for(int i=maxIdx-1; i>=0; i--){
  cost += a[i] - h;
  if(h>0)
    h--;
}

// COST ON RIGHT SIDE
h = maxHeight-1;
for(int i=maxIdx+1; i<n; i++){
  cost += a[i] - h;
  if(h>0)
    h--;
}
return cost;
}
```

This DP solution takes O(n) time. One can argue that this DP solution is not better than the brute-force because it is taking more memory. There is a trade-off between time and memory in the two solutions.

In the next example also the brute-force does not have recursion and is not exponential.

Example 8.5: Longest Arithmetic Progression (AP) Sequence in an array

Given an array arr of integers, find the length of the longest arithmetic subsequence in the array. Example 5.5 define what a subsequence is. A sequence s is an AP sequence if s[i+1]-s[i] is same for all possible values of i(0 < i <= s.length-1). For example, if the given array is

int[] arr = {10, 5, 17, 7, 2, 4, 1, 8}

Then the output should 4 that represent the length of the following AP sequence with common difference d=3;

{10, 7, 4, 1}

If the array is

{12, 8, 4, 0}

Then the whole array is an AP sequence with common difference d=4.

Brute-Force has no Recursion

The brute-force logic is to pick two elements from the array and find the difference between them. There are n(n+1) ways of picking two elements from an array of size n. For each pair, find the longest AP sequence from the remaining elements that have the same common difference as elements in the pair. For example, for the following input array,

```
int[] arr = {10, 5, 17, 7, 2, 4, 1, 8}
```

pick first two elements (10,5) as a pair and then find the elements from rest of the array that follows this AP, the next element in this series should be 0, then -5, -10, etc. Pick the first 0 that you find, then pick the first -5 following the 0, etc.

There are n*(n-1) ways of picking a pair, and for each pair, there is a linear time single traversal of the array to find the AP sequence. For pair (10, 5), the next element must be 0. If there are more than one 0's in the array following 5, picking the first 0 will give us the most optimal result.

```
static int maxAPSeqLen(int[] a) {
  if(a.length <= 2){
    return a.length;
  }
  int maxLen = 2;
  for(int i=0; i<a.length; i++){
    for(int j=i+1; j<a.length; j++){
      int cd = a[j] - a[i];   //COMMON DIFF
      int lastNum = a[j];
      int len = 2;
      for(int k=j+1; k<a.length; k++){
        if(a[k] == lastNum+cd){
          len++;
          lastNum = a[k];
          maxLen = getMax(maxLen, len);
        }
      }
    }
```

```
        }
    }
    return maxLen;
}
```

Code: 8.1

This solution is not recursive but there are overlapping subproblems, you may be searching inside the same subarray with the same common difference multiple times.

Memoization

Code 8.1 has overlapping subproblems that we should not be solving multiple times. What data structure should we use to cache the results of subproblems?

We find and save the length of the longest AP sequence for each pair. A two-dimensional array appears to be the obvious choice for cache. However, it may be better to store the number of elements in the AP series based on common difference, so a HashMap may be better with key in the HashMap being the common difference. For every element in the array, find the maximum length of AP series that this element can has with a particular common difference. The number of common differences will be finite based on other elements in the array (for every pair involving this element, either the number in an existing AP series attached with this number will increase, or a new AP series will be added to this number).

Therefore, use a HashMap (Dictionary) for every element in the array. The key of HashMap is the common-difference and value is the length of longest AP sequence with that difference. Essentially, we will maintain a HashMap, instead of an array for each element (and array for each element means a two-dimensional array overall).

Dynamic Programming Solution

In the following Dynamic Programming solution, we store the number of elements in the AP sequence of the difference between two elements of the pair for each pair.

For each element in the array, we maintain a HashMap where key is the difference of that element with other elements in the array and value is the number of elements in the AP. For example, the HashMap of first element,

10 in the given array will have following Keys,

Key	Meaning
5	This key represents the difference of 10 and 5
-7	This key represents the difference of 10 and 17
3	This key represents the difference of 10 and 7
8	This key represents the difference of 10 and 2
6	This key represents the difference of 10 and 4
9	This key represents the difference of 10 and 1
2	This key represents the difference of 10 and 8

Values of the above keys in the HashMap will be the number of elements in the AP sequence with a difference equal to the corresponding key when the sequence starts from 10. Following diagram shows the HashMap of each element of the array.

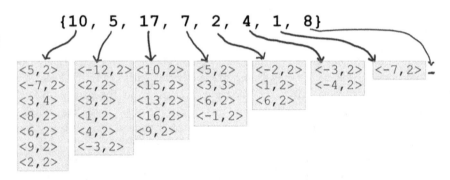

HashMap of each element in the above diagram consider all other elements following it. However, in DP, we will examine the logic in the opposite direction and consider all the elements before each element.

For element at index i, find the difference of a[i] with each element before it, and for each element see how many elements with the same difference exist in the HashMap of that element while populating the HashMap of the current element, a[i]. Following code is the DP solution of this problem,

```java
public int longestAPSeqLength(int[] a) {
  int n= a.length;
  HashMap<Integer, Integer>[] dp = new HashMap[n];
  for(int i=0; i<n; i++)
    dp[i] = new HashMap<Integer, Integer>();
  int maxVal = 2;
```

```
    for(int i=1; i<n; i++)
    {
      for(int j=0; j<i; j++)
      {
        int diff = a[i] - a[j];
        int val = 1;
        if(dp[j].containsKey(diff))
          val = dp[j].get(diff);
        dp[i].put(diff, val+1);
        if(val+1 > maxVal)
          maxVal = val+1;
      }
    }
    return maxVal;
}
```

The above DP solution takes $O(n^2)$ time.

Example 8.6 (Maximum Sum Subarray): Given an array of integers, write a function that returns the sum of subarray having a maximum sum. For example,

Input Array: {-2, -3, 4, -1, -2, 1, 5, -3}
Output: 7 (Sum of **4, -1, -2, 1, 5**)

Note that the subarray is a contiguous chunk of an array.

The brute-force algorithm for this question, or any other question related to continuous subarray is to have two loops and consider all possible intervals (i,j) of the array, for all valid values of i and j such that i<=j as shown in Code 2.5. Following code use this approach:

```
int maxSubArraySum(int[] a){
  int maxSum = 0;
  for(int i=0; i<a.length; i++){
    for(int j=i; j<a.length; j++){
      int sum = getSubArraySum(a, i, j);
      if(sum > maxSum)
        maxSum = sum;
    }
```

```
  }
  return maxSum;
}
```

The function `getSubArraySum` finds the sum of a subarray when the start and end point of the subarray is given.

```
int getSubArraySum(int[] a, int s, int e){
  int sum = 0;
  for(int i=s; i<=e; i++)
    sum += a[i];
  return sum;
}
```

This solution takes $O(n^3)$ time. This can be slightly improved by removing the not computing the sum again from i to (j-1) inside the inner loop.

```
static int maxSubArraySum(int[] a){
  int maxSum = 0;
  for(int i=0; i<a.length; i++){
    int tempSum=0; //FOR SUM OF ELEMENTS FROM i TO j
    for(int j=i; j<a.length; j++){
      tempSum += a[j];
      if(tempSum > maxSum)
        maxSum = tempSum;
    }
  }
  return maxSum;
}
```

This code takes $O(n^2)$ time. If all of the array's elements are negative, this algorithm will return 0. If that is not acceptable, we can add another loop before the return statement to handle the case where `maxSum` is 0 and set it to the largest value in the array.

Kadane's Algorithm

In this approach we scan the array only once and at each point compute the maximum sum of subarrays ending at that point. Maintain two variables,

```
int maxSumEndingHere = 0;
```

```
int maxSumSoFar = 0;
```

Loop for each element in the array and change the two variables using the following logic:

```
maxSumEndingHere = maxSumEndingHere + a[i]
if(maxSumEndingHere < 0)
    maxSumEndingHere = 0
if(maxSumSoFar < maxSumEndingHere)
    maxSumSoFar = maxSumEndingHere
```

Following is the complete code:

```
static int maxSubArraySum(int[] a){
   int maxSumSoFar = 0;
   int maxSumEndingHere = 0;

   for (int i=0; i<a.length; i++){
     maxSumEndingHere = maxSumEndingHere + a[i];

     if (maxSumEndingHere < 0)
       maxSumEndingHere = 0;

     if (maxSumSoFar < maxSumEndingHere )
       maxSumSoFar = maxSumEndingHere ;
   }
   return maxSumSoFar;
}
```

The idea behind Kadane's algorithm is to add any subarray with a net positive sum. The subarray will be ignored only if the sum is negative. This function takes $O(n)$ time and is an improvement over the previous one. If we call this function for the following array

```
{-2, -3, 4, -1, -2, 1, 5, -3}
```

Then the intermediate values of maxSumEndingHere and maxSumSoFar variables are as shown in the table below:

i	maxSumEndingHere	maxSumSoFar
0	0	0
1	0	0
2	4	4
3	3	4
4	1	4
5	2	4
6	7	7
7	4	7

Note the optimal substructure property, to find the `maxSubArraySum` for n elements we need to find `maxSubArraySum` of n-1 elements.

This is one of the few examples of dynamic programming where brute force solution is non-recursive and it comes easily. This is not the best example to demonstrate dynamic programming.

We have not discussed the recursive solution to `maxSubArraySum`, The recursion is defined as;
```
M(n) = max(M(n-1) + A[n], 0)
```

Where `M` is the function, `maxSubArraySum` and `A` is the array.

The core solution of this question actually uses the include-exclude logic where we see whether the current element will be included in the subarray or not. But this is one of the rare dynamic programming problems where the recursion is not intuitive and DP solutions come more naturally to you without the recursion itself. Even in case of Fibonacci numbers, there are people who learn the DP solution directly without the recursion.

ACKNOWLEDGMENTS

We'd like to thank everyone who helped make the first edition of this book such a huge success. Writing a book was never a planned move. It was just a reflection of how we understood, taught, and approached Dynamic Programming problems.

Much has changed in the last few years. Coding interviews are now common, and many coding portals, such as leetcode, have sprung up on the internet. An update of this book was long overdue. With the blessings of Lord Shiva and our Gurus, we present to you this new edition.

We've taught over 5,000 students in the last few years, and each interaction has improved our understanding of problem-solving. We thank all our students who are now among the best performers of top IT companies. We wish you all many more successes.

Time spent working on this book was stolen from the share of family and friends. Thanks to all of them for their patience.

Like a yajna, book writing is incomplete without the blessings of the elders. Thank you, Mom and Dad!

www.ingramcontent.com/pod-product-compliance
Lightning Source LLC
LaVergne TN
LVHW051234050326
832903LV00028B/2393